THE GOD
GROOVE

ALSO BY DAVID RITZ

BIOGRAPHY

Respect: The Life of Aretha Franklin

Before You Judge Me: Michael Jackson's Last Days (co-written with Tavis Smiley)

My Journey with Maya Angelou (co-written with Tavis Smiley)

Divided Soul: The Life of Marvin Gaye

Faith in Time: The Life of Jimmy Scott

Death of a King: The Real Story of Dr. Martin Luther King Jr.'s Final Year (co-written with Tavis Smiley)

AUTOBIOGRAPHY

Brother Ray (co-written with Ray Charles)

Inside My Life (co-written with Smokey Robinson)

Blues All Around Me (co-written with B. B. King)

Rage to Survive (co-written with Etta James)

The Brothers (co-written with the Neville Brothers)

Rhythm and the Blues (co-written with Jerry Wexler)

Aretha: From These Roots (co-written with Aretha Franklin)

Howling at the Moon (co-written with Walter Yetnikoff)

Guillaume: A Life (co-written with Robert Guillaume)

Reach! (co-written with Laila Ali)

Inside Power (co-written with Gary Sheffield)

Grace After Midnight (co-written with Felicia "Snoop" Pearson)

Journey of a Thousand Miles (co-written with Lang Lang)

Rickles' Book (co-written with Don Rickles)

Rickles' Letters (co-written with Don Rickles)

Hound Dog (co-written with Jerry Leiber and Mike Stoller)

We'll Be Here for the Rest of Our Lives (co-written with Paul Shaffer)

The Adventures of Grandmaster Flash (co-written with Grandmaster Flash)

What I Know for Sure (co-written with Tavis Smiley)

Brother West (co-written with Cornel West)

I Was Born This Way (co-written with Carl Bean)

Love Brought Me Back (co-written with Natalie Cole)

True You (co-written with Janet Jackson)

Not Dead and Not for Sale (co-written with Scott Weiland)

A Moment in Time (co-written with Ralph Branca)

A Woman Like Me (co-written with Bettye LaVette)

Sinner's Creed (co-written with Scott Stapp)

When I Left Home (co-written with Buddy Guy)

Balance (co-written with Nik Wallenda)

Glow (co-written with Rick James)

Rocks (co-written with Joe Perry)

It's a Long Story: My Life (co-written with Willie Nelson)

After the Dance: My Life with Marvin Gaye
(co-written with Jan Gaye)

An Outlaw and a Lady (co-written with Jessi Colter)

FICTION

Search for Happiness

The Man Who Brought the Dodgers Back to Brooklyn

Blues Notes Under a Green Felt Hat

Barbells and Saxophones

Family Blood

Take It Off! Take It All Off!

Passion Flowers

Sanctified Blues (co-written with Mable John)

Stay Out of the Kitchen (co-written with Mable John)

Love Tornado (co-written with Mable John)

Power and Beauty (co-written with T. I. Harris)

Trouble and Triumph (co-written with T. I. Harris)

Pretty Paper (co-written with Willie Nelson)

INSPIRATIONAL

Messengers: African American Ministers and Gospel

THE GOD GROOVE

A BLUES JOURNEY TO FAITH

DAVID RITZ

HOWARD BOOKS

ATRIA

NEW YORK
LONDON
TORONTO
SYDNEY
NEW DELHI

ATRIA

An Imprint of Simon & Schuster, Inc.
1230 Avenue of the Americas
New York, NY 10020

First Howard Books/Atria Books hardcover edition July 2019

HOWARD BOOKS/ATRIA BOOKS and colophon are trademarks of Simon & Schuster, Inc.

For information about special discounts for bulk purchases, please contact Simon
& Schuster Special Sales at 1-866-506-1949 or business@simonandschuster.com.

The Simon & Schuster Speakers Bureau can bring authors to your live event.
For more information or to book an event, contact the Simon & Schuster Speakers
Bureau at 1-866-248-3049 or visit our website at www.simonspeakers.com.

Interior design by Michelle Marchese

Manufactured in the United States of America

10 9 8 7 6 5 4 3 2 1

Library of Congress Cataloging-in-Publication Data

Names: Ritz, David, author.
Title: The God groove : a blues journey to faith / by David Ritz.
Description: First Howard Books hardcover edition. | New York : Howard Books,
    2019.
Identifiers: LCCN 2018041790 (print) | LCCN 2018052804 (ebook) | ISBN
    9781501177170 (eBook) | ISBN 9781501177156 (hardcover)
Subjects: LCSH: Musicians—Religious life. | Christian life. | Ritz, David.
Classification: LCC ML385 (ebook) | LCC ML385 .R58 2019 (print) | DDC 780.92
    [B]—dc23
LC record available at https://lccn.loc.gov/2018041790

ISBN 978-1-5011-7715-6
ISBN 978-1-5011-7717-0 (ebook)

For Roberta,
wonderful wife, wonderful writer

INTRODUCTION

A T AGE SEVENTY-FIVE, I'm writing a book that has been brewing for a long while. I've castigated myself for not getting to it sooner but now realize that this extended gestation was necessary. I had to get over a deep fear of not being able to make sense of my coming to faith.

I'm still afraid, but on a deeper level that fear, while not defeated, is tempered by curiosity. I'm curious to see what I'm going to write. Because jazz is my creative model, I'm an improviser. I'm making this up as I go along. I see it as a long solo.

The fear that my solo will be boring and convoluted is still there. But I'm motivated by the belief that rather than run from my fears, I need to walk—or write—my way through them. If I don't, my fears will do more than block me; they'll rule me.

Looking back, I see that a joyful, irrepressible groove has always led me on. The blues groove. The jazz groove. The gospel groove. The rhythm groove I could never resist. It's this groove that turned around my life and allowed me to become a ghostwriter.

As a ghost chasing a groove, I caught up with artists whose music enchanted me. I helped give each of those artists a literary voice. Yet many of those artists led me to another voice that I had never expected to hear: the voice of God. Those artists taught me that, ironically, I had always been hearing that voice. The voice was in their music. The voice was in their groove. The ever-changing voice spoke in shouts and whispers, dispensing wisdom about ways to heal the human heart.

BROTHER RAY

N 1976 I WAS a thirty-two-year-old ad man living in Dallas with my wife, Roberta, and twin two-year-old daughters, Alison and Jessica. I was looking to get out of a business that bored me to death. I needed a new life. I needed to meet Ray Charles.

As a boy, I became obsessed with Ray Charles's voice. I loved how it shocked and soothed and cracked and screamed. No pent-up emotions. He got it all out there. His blues roots anchored every song he sang. His blues transformed my sense of beauty. Driving his blues was a groove that drove me. He held some mystery I had to uncover.

I ran to the library to see if there was a biography of Ray. None. Great. Right then and there, I decided to write one.

Of course, I'd need his cooperation. I had to convince him to join forces with me in sculpting the story of his life.

I pursued Ray Charles hard. I had a head of steam. For the previous five years, I had studied the art of selling. I knew the ins and outs of signing up a new client—listen to their particular needs, express your eagerness in promoting their product, expound on your creative abilities, and then gently but firmly close the deal. I viewed Ray as a potential client. I wanted his business more than any business I had ever wanted before. I knew that obtaining that business would change my life. My motivation was off the charts.

My motivation was also fueled by my heavy use of marijuana. As my interest in advertising waned, my pot smoking increased. Unlike many smokers, I never experienced weed as a soporific. Much like cocaine, pot overstimulated me. If my normal speed was fifty mph, weed cranked me up to a hundred. It served to embolden me to do things I might not otherwise do. Making cold calls to Ray Charles's Los Angeles office was one such thing.

Those calls got me nowhere. The receptionist flatly said that he took no calls. I asked to speak to his manager. For what purpose? I wanted to enlist Mr. Charles's cooperation in writing his biography. I was put on hold. The manager told the operator to say Mr. Charles had no such interest. What was the manager's name? Joe Adams. I had heard of

Joe Adams. He had been a jazz and R & B deejay on LA radio in the forties and fifties. He had been singer Lena Horne's emcee. He had also enjoyed success as a film actor, appearing in Otto Preminger's *Carmen Jones* and playing Frank Sinatra's psychiatrist in *The Manchurian Candidate*. Now, as Ray's number two man, he had a ruthless reputation.

"He's Ray's eyes," said saxophonist David "Fathead" Newman, one of Ray's former sidemen, whom I had met in Dallas when I was a teenager exploring African American neighborhoods in search of good music.

"He doesn't let anyone get too close to Ray," added James Clay, another jazz saxophonist I'd befriended. He'd gone on the road with Ray.

"Can you put in a good word for me?" I asked both of them.

They said they'd try, but it was tough getting through.

I wrote Joe Adams long letters that remained unanswered. I called him many times without a single response. Yet something told me to make a bolder move.

I flew to Los Angeles and showed up at Ray's office. He owned a nondescript two-story pale-green building on Washington Boulevard, a few miles west of downtown. The area was a mix of decaying houses from the twenties and businesses selling restaurant supplies, tires, liquor, and linoleum. "RPM" was written on the outside of Ray's edifice:

Recording, Publishing and Management. The bottom floor
had windows and was leased to a government agency. The
top floor housed Ray's offices and recording studio. It had no
windows. I'd later learn that Ray, with no use for windows,
ordered the architect to design it that way to cut costs.

A suspended staircase led to the second floor. The waiting room was small: walls decorated with posters of Ray, copies of *Billboard* magazine on the coffee room table, the floor
covered in white shag carpet. The receptionist sat behind a
glass window. I said that I was there to see Joe Adams. Was
he expecting me? No. Wait one minute. Sorry, Mr. Adams
is not available. I returned the next day. And the day after.
And then the day after that. On the fourth day, Adams finally
came out to see me.

"You're a pain" were his first words. But I suppose because he was curious, he invited me into this office.

He was a tall African American with light skin, thin mustache, piercing eyes, and a deep baritone voice. His deejay
chops were on full display. He spoke with perfect diction. No
street jargon. He wore a black double-breasted pinstriped
suit, black shirt, and white tie. I saw him as a cross between
Cab Calloway and a Broadway gangster from *Guys and Dolls*.
His office walls were painted black, and his furniture—the
high chair behind his desk and the twin guest chairs on either side—was covered in cherry-red leather. Because there

were no windows, the black-and-red motif took on a demonic tone, especially when Adams opened his suit jacket to reveal a shoulder holster containing a pistol.

"You say you're a biographer," he said. "What are your credentials?"

I explained that this would be my first book, but I had brought some of my published articles. I also mentioned my experience as a copywriter. He was not impressed.

"You lack the qualifications," he said. "If Mr. Charles were interested in a biographer, I'd be loath to recommend any author other than one with a distinguished body of work."

I started pleading my case, saying that if only I could speak to Ray himself . . .

"That's it, Mr. Ritz. You pushed your way in here. Now it's time to ease your way out."

I sulked for a day. I was staying in a cheap motel in the sketchy neighborhood around Ray's office. I thought about packing it in and going home. This would be far from the first time that I'd felt the sting of rejection from a potential client. You can't win 'em all. But somehow the clichés of failed salesmanship didn't sink in. I lit a joint, leaned back in bed, and thought it through: I hadn't been rejected by the client; I'd been rejected by the client's *manager*. Big difference. I had a gnawing feeling that were I to meet Ray, he'd like me, just as other bluesmen I had interviewed for magazine profiles—

Jimmy Reed, Lightnin' Hopkins, and John Lee Hooker—had liked me. He'd see the passion behind my purpose. He'd see the need to document his history accurately and lovingly. He'd get me.

But how to get to him?

I couldn't put in another call to his office. I couldn't try for another meeting with Adams. Those doors were shut tight. I needed to make an end run. How?

I knew Ray was a reader. In several interviews, he spoke about his knowledge of the Bible and certain novels he had enjoyed. I also reasoned that he was probably the only one in his office who knew braille. So what if I wrote to him in braille? I called Western Union and asked whether telegrams could be sent in braille. For a nominal fee, yes. That's all I needed to hear.

Each day for five straight days I sent him a lengthy telegram in braille. I confessed my unmitigated love of his music, my obsession with his sound since I'd discovered him as a child, my determination to honor the complexity of his story. I wrote that it was important for him to be candid. The world knew about his heroin addiction, and that issue had to be addressed head-on. The world knew about his many women, and that too had to be a central theme. I also argued that if he didn't write his history, someone else would—and that someone, without his cooperation, might well get it wrong. This

was his chance to tell his story his way. I mentioned my friendship with Fathead Newman and James Clay. I ended each telegram with the phone and room numbers of my motel.

In this pre–cell phone era, I waited in my dingy room for
the phone to ring. I stared at that phone for hours, for days.
I willed it to ring, and then, at ten o'clock on Thursday night,
it did.

"Ritz?" asked a voice deep and raw.

"Yes."

"Brother Ray. You free?"

"Now?"

"Right now. Go to the back of the building, hit the buzzer,
and I'll let you in."

I was there in under five minutes, my heart fluttering. I
pushed a button, and the door buzzed open. I walked up a
flight of stairs that led to a door. I knocked.

"Come in."

I walked into a pitch-dark room.

"Oh, sorry," he said. "I forgot you're one of those cats who
need light."

The light came on to reveal Ray sitting behind a mas-
sive recording console. He was wearing a blue silk shirt and
tight-fitting brown trousers. His wraparound shades were
firmly in place. His hands fluttered over the faders, knobs,
and buttons.

"Gimme a sec," he said before studying a Wurlitzer piano solo he'd just recorded. I wanted to say that it sounded great, but I figured I'd better button up.

He listened to the solo several times before turning off the tape.

"Sit down," he said, pointing to a chair next to his. "I wanna get a look at the cat that's keeping Western Union in business."

His chuckle allowed me to laugh.

"Figured it was the only way to get through," I said.

"Figured right."

"Hope I didn't anger anyone."

"Only one you gotta worry 'bout angerin' 'round here is me. Telegrams didn't get me angry. They showed me you could write—and you like writing."

"I love it."

"Me too. Not book writing. But music writing. Even though I don't got to—I got people who'll do it for me—I still write a big band arrangement least once a year. Just to make sure I can still do it."

From there we started talking about big bands—Duke Ellington and Count Basie—and piano players—Erroll Garner and Oscar Peterson. We spoke about the blues, the country blues he heard back in Georgia, and the big-city blues he heard when he came to LA. We talked about the Bible, and why he read it with skepticism. He wanted to know if I had ever read Norman Mailer. The question shocked me, but the answer was yes. Ray had just read an article by Mailer in *Playboy* and was wondering which of his books he should read. I joked that everyone said they read *Playboy* just for the articles, but in Ray's case that was the truth. "The gospel truth," Ray added.

The more we talked, the easier the banter. His energy was extraordinary. His language was a mix of backcountry bawdiness and big-city slick. He called me "love." I later learned he called many men "love," as in "All right, love, good talking to you, but I gotta run." He pulled out a joint, the fattest one I'd ever seen—he said he rolled it himself—stuck it at the end of a cigarette holder, and, cupping his hands to catch all the smoke, inhaled it before asking whether I wanted a hit. I did. He liked laughing, and when he did, he'd sometimes fall to the floor. In making points, he'd slap his knees and, with his fist, beat his chest. His gesticulations were quirky and endearing. His mood, at least during this initial meeting, was ebullient.

He mentioned that he had, in fact, gotten calls from Fathead and Clay, who each put in a good word for me. "I was sure-enough surprised to hear from them," he said. "They're heavy cats and ain't big talkers."

We talked about the book itself. Ray wanted to know how

it would work. I said my main job was to interview him and write the text. He also wanted to know whether I'd need to talk to other people. I said yes and wondered if that bothered him. "The truth's the truth," he said. "Truth never bothers me. This book don't have to make me look good. It just has to *be* me."

We left on great terms. I told him I was heading to New York to find a literary agent who would facilitate finding a publisher. He thought that was a good idea. We shook hands, he gave me his private number, and that was it.

"One last question," I said.

"Shoot."

"I didn't get off on the right foot with your manager."

"Look, love," said Ray. "It's my book, not his."

And with that, he turned his attention back to the recording console.

High as a kite, I ran back to my room, called Roberta, and said it was on. She was thrilled for me. I couldn't sleep all night and, in the morning, drove over to Canter's Delicatessen on Fairfax Avenue, the heart of a middle-class Jewish neighborhood. The down-home feeling brought me back to my childhood in New York City and Newark, New Jersey, except that it was January, and instead of freezing to death, I was bathed in seventy-five-degree sunshine. I called Roberta again and said, "I think we should move here." Happy to hear the words—my wife never liked Dallas and tolerated it only because of me—her only question was "How soon?"

A week later, I was in New York interviewing agents. They told me to come back when I had a written contract from Ray. Because I had nothing on paper, and because I had no book credits, they had no interest in representing me. Only one did: Aaron Priest. He sensed my tenacity and agreed to take me on. On one issue, though, he had pushback. My idea was to write a biography. In college, I had admired Richard Ellmann's books on James Joyce and W. B. Yeats. They were my models.

Aaron argued that an autobiography would mean more money. That was fine—I wanted money—but that meant I'd be a ghostwriter, not a biographer. Biographers win Pulitzer Prizes. Ghostwriters don't. I wanted a Pulitzer Prize.

"Let me ask you this," said tough-talking Aaron. "Which book would you rather read: a biography of Ray written by some egghead, or a book about Ray's life written in his own voice?"

Thinking of Billie Holiday's *Lady Sings the Blues* and *The Autobiography of Malcolm X*, I answered, "A book written in his own voice."

"*Then forget the book you think you should write and instead write the book you want to read.*"

That single statement altered my career.

I flew back to Los Angeles to get Ray's reaction. He agreed. Put the book in his voice. Let him tell his own story his own way.

The wait for signed contracts took months. Beyond the fact that Ray was touring Europe and Asia, I was convinced that Joe Adams was undercutting the deal. I was in heavy paranoia until, six months after we had met, Ray called to say he was ready to sign.

Roberta, Jessica, Alison, and I moved to an LA neighborhood only twenty minutes from Ray's office.

The work began, but what was the work? He talked, I taped, I transcribed the tapes, but what then? How do I turn talk into prose?

I took first things first. I got Ray to talk—and not talk superficially, but talk in depth, talk about feelings, talk about fears, talk tenderly, and talk angrily. Talk, talk, talk.

Okay. Now I had these talking tapes. What next?

I typed every single word by myself because, as a novice know-nothing ghostwriter, I was scared of missing something, and, even worse, I was scared that I'd misrepresent the man that I, his literary surrogate, was pretending to be.

I soon discovered that the transcriptions were helpful and the transcriptions were useless. They were helpful because of the information they contained. They were useless because his voice was nowhere to be found in them. His literal words, typed out on the page, did not equal his authentic voice.

Why?

Because readers don't read with their ears. They read with their eyes. Eyes hear differently from ears. The eyes and the eyes alone hear the silent sound of seemingly spoken words. Thus, the faithful translation from what is said to what is read is a trick, a ruse.

So how, then, *do* you capture a voice?

Instinctively. Creatively. Artfully.

I slowly saw that, in ghosting, I was creating art. I realized that you learn to talk before you sing, and that, in listening to Ray's conversation style, I heard the root of his singing style. The way he grunted and groaned. How he cut off words was how he cut off notes. His idiosyncratic syntax was carried from his speech to his music. Therefore, if I were to faithfully re-create his voice, I too would be making music. I was able to translate his musical groove into a literary groove.

In his own intuitive way, Ray Charles, an artist both spontaneous and exacting, helped school me in the ghostwriting craft. He saw, for example, in the section describing his childhood that his voice was too confident. "As a little boy," he said, "I was afraid a lot of the time. You have to make me sound afraid."

"But when you told me those stories," I said, "you didn't sound afraid."

"Look," he said, "you're the writer. You gotta feel me, or it ain't gonna work. Once you feel me, you'll know what to write."

Those were the words I typed out and looked at every morning as I crafted the book.

"Once you feel me, you'll know what to write."

A voice feels right or it feels wrong. A voice feels fake or it feels real.

"It's a riff," said Ray. "Like when I riff on piano. Only it's a riff with words, not notes. Get my riffs right, and you got me right."

Before I turned in the book, my editor was concerned that I wouldn't get it right. She asked me whether, in my relationship with Ray, race was an issue. I wasn't sure what she meant.

"Do you think he's less comfortable talking to you because you're white?" she asked.

I thought enough of the question to ask Ray.

He laughed. "Love," he said, "I couldn't care less."

Ray's attitude was reflected in every African American artist I worked with—from blues singer Etta James to hip-hop pioneer Grandmaster Flash. I didn't have to explain that I was coming from a place of deep admiration. They felt it. They felt my determination to get their riffs right.

My riffing also included research. I made lengthy research trips to Ray's hometown of Greenville, Florida, and
the school for the blind and deaf where he traveled half-
way across the state to study in St. Augustine. I spoke to his
friends and a few of his teachers. Most described him as re-
markably self-reliant but also willfully self-centered.

Ray was eager to hear about the people I'd interviewed.
He handled the personal criticism I conveyed with interest
rather than annoyance. Our relationship remained good, but
not without trying moments. It took a few painful incidents
to see the limits of the familiarity I'd cultivated with Ray.
Once, for example, he invited me to a session when he was
singing. It was the middle of the night, a time when he liked
to work. Having smoked one of his jumbo joints, he was in a
mellow mood. By then, six months into the project, I thought
I understood those moods. Though Ray had kicked heroin
cold turkey back in the sixties, he had replaced it with other
stimulants. Every morning, he had his first drink of the day:
a huge mug composed of equal parts black coffee and Bols
gin mixed with five heaping spoonfuls of sugar. He imbibed
that cocktail four times every day—ten o'clock in the morning, noon, and two and four in the afternoon—before, at six,
turning to pot to take off the edge. I tried the gin-coffee-sugar
drink under the guise of "research," but couldn't stomach it.
When it came to weed, though, I had no problem.

During this late-night recording session, when he was experimenting with a version of "Oh, What a Beautiful Morning," there was a pause between takes when I asked him whether he had ever listened to the original soundtrack of the song's source, *Oklahoma!*

Ray turned to me furiously. "Look here, man, you ain't here to distract. You're here to shut up and listen!"

It took me a few days to recover from the sting.

Another time, we were flying together to New York, where he was to appear on *Saturday Night Live*, then in its third season. It was 1977. I was especially excited because I had arranged the date. I'd become close to Jerry Wexler, one of the owners of Atlantic Records responsible for Ray's breakthrough hits in the fifties. *SNL* producer Lorne Michaels had asked Wexler if he had a way to get to Ray because Joe Adams was not returning his calls. Knowing I was with Ray nearly every night, Wexler prevailed on me. I said I'd do it if, on the show, Michaels would reunite Ray's original small band that included my friend Fathead Newman. Ray liked the idea of playing with his old buddies on TV but had one caveat: he wanted to host as well. When the issue of cue cards came up, Ray said, "If I can memorize music, I can memorize a few comedy lines." Thus, the deal was done, and I got to go along for the ride.

Sitting next to Ray in first class, I figured I had six hours to interview him. My passion for interviewing had grown exponentially. As soon as we buckled in, I whipped out my tape recorder and started asking questions.

"Get that thing out of my face," Ray said scornfully. "Right now I wouldn't talk to my mama if she popped out of the grave."

He then put down his head and slept until we touched ground in New York. As a host, he was dazzling. Didn't fluff a single line. It was an exhilarating weekend. I got to mingle with the original cast: John Belushi, Dan Aykroyd, Gilda Radner, and the rest. Pot smoking and cocaine snorting, in which I partook, was part of their creative process. (Ray, by the way, didn't like coke. "Does nothing for me," he said, "and costs too much.") At the after-party, I met Claude Nobs, head of the Montreux Jazz Festival, who asked if I could convince Ray to play with this same original small band in Switzerland. I said I'd try. "If you can do it," said Claude, "I'll fly you over with Ray."

Ray was willing, and we flew to Europe together. In Montreux, we learned that Claude had, in fact, hired Ray's original horn players, including Fathead, but, in order to save money, he'd arranged to use Dizzy Gillespie's rhythm section to supplement the band. Ray was furious but, after a nasty confrontation with Claude, went along with the program.

Ray was murder on drummers. His sense of rhythm was ever changing, and he expected the drummer to follow along. "Watch my feet, baby!" he'd admonish. "Always watch my

feet!" His stomping was the drummer's only guide. Mickey
Roker, Dizzy's drummer, was a bebop great but hadn't played
with Ray before. Onstage, in front of the public, Ray chastised Mickey unmercifully. Dizzy was furious. "I would have
hit Ray over the head with my trumpet," he told me afterward, "but I didn't wanna ruin my trumpet."

Ray's moods were more than mercurial; they were often
manic, but in a singular Ray way. When it came to discussing
his sexual history, he was forthcoming. He spoke of his fondness for orgies and his guileless attitude about multi-affairs and
one-night stands. His favorite analogy invoked the barnyard: "I
see many chickens, but one rooster." His chauvinism was hard-
core, and he had no reservations about saying so in his book.
While I was working with him, though, he kept his current lovers out of my sight. He never got specific. Only after *Brother
Ray* was published in 1978, for example, did I learn that he'd
had a decades-long relationship with Arlette Kotchounian,
a French songwriter. Their son, Vincent, was born while we
were writing the book, a fact Ray never mentioned.

His ability to compartmentalize was nearly as formidable as his ability to make music. He had families scattered
around several countries and would tend to them whenever
his schedule allowed. Yet none of these women—nor his
heavy drinking or daily pot smoking—interfered with Ray's
most ferocious compulsion: work. Work involved recording

and touring. He liked earning, he liked living parsimoniously, and he liked saving money. Of all his addictions, the most powerful crosscurrent was where music met money.

Naturally, this fascinated me. As a veteran of advertising, I had struggled with the commerce-versus-art dichotomy. Ray described his greatest innovation—taking sacred church songs and infusing them with sexual lyrics—as an act of blatant marketing.

"I knew those church rhythms were hot," he said, "and I knew they would sell. I also thought that the superstition around those gospels was bull. The church said, 'If you take our music and give it to the devil, God will strike you down.' Well, I'm still standing."

As we delved deeper into the subject of religion, I got more personal. I told him how bored I was at the Jewish services I attended as a kid. He asked what they were like. I said I found them mainly intellectual.

"That's cause y'all are chilled out," he said. "Y'all don't have to jump up and down."

But what about Jesus?

"I wonder why Jesus couldn't convince all the Jews that he was the Messiah," he said. "After all, he was a Jew. They were his people. And the Jews, the folks who were there at the beginning of the Bible, didn't turn away from the truth. Worries me that Jesus wasn't able to convince the very people he came from."

Ray claimed to believe in a supreme being, but wondered why that being needed so much praise.

"Don't like it when folks say they're God fearing," he explained. "There's only one thing I'm really scared of."

"What's that?"

"Cancer."

During my time with Ray, I had a deep fear of flying. It started years earlier when, on a trip from Buffalo to New York, the jet was hit by lightning. No damage, but panic in my heart.

Ray helped cure me. On several trips with him—both on commercial jets and his own propeller plane—we flew through some hair-raising storms. Sitting next to him, though, I had no fear. I absorbed his survivor energy. My proximity to him provided all the protection I needed. He wasn't afraid of God, and, besides, God wouldn't dare strike down his plane.

At the Dorothy Chandler Pavilion, a fancy concert hall in Los Angeles, I wondered whether he was afraid when a man in the audience ran up onstage and embraced him. He was a fan who meant no harm; he just wanted to love on Ray. Backstage in his dressing room, I asked Ray about the incident. "Wasn't afraid," he said, "just surprised. You expect that might happen at a juke joint, but not the Dorothy Chandler."

Next morning, Joe Adams, who had not attended the

concert but whose antipathy for me remained intense, called me to his office.

"You're out," he said. "You're fired."

"For what?"

"For bothering Ray after the incident last night. That was the time to leave him alone. He needed his privacy. And you rushed in there with your infernal questions. You're driving him crazy. We're looking for another writer."

That made no sense. Never reticent about his true feelings, Ray had displayed no displeasure with me. That afternoon, I called him to see if our late-night interview was canceled.

"Why should it be?" he asked.

I didn't answer, but when I arrived, I told him that Joe had fired me.

Ray sat quietly for a minute before picking up the phone. By then, it was three in the morning.

"Joe," he said, "David and I are sitting here, and we're hungry. We want Chinese. I want barbecue ribs. How 'bout you, David?"

"Pork fried rice."

"Ribs and pork fried rice, and pick up some Cokes. And don't forget the forks, knives, and napkins."

Forty-five minutes later, Joe showed up with containers of food.

"Lay out the stuff," said Ray, "then go home. I'll call you if we need anything else."

That was it. Ray never said another word about the incident, and neither did Joe.

WHEN I COMPLETED a draft of the book, Ray proved to be an astute editor, pointing out where I'd caught or missed his true voice. He modified many of my metaphors and added a few of his own. When it was complete, he read it in braille straight through and gave a five-word critique: "I like it. It's me."

The book came out, reviews were good, sales were brisk, and I thought my career was made. Surely James Brown or Stevie Wonder would be calling me. Surely Aretha Franklin, to whom Ray had introduced me after one of his concerts, would reply to my letter, asking that I collaborate on her book.

Instead, no one called. Not James, not Stevie, not Aretha. After the publication of a successful book, I was shocked to learn that nothing had changed. I had to keep hustling.

DON'T
STUTTER

WHEN I WAS SEVEN YEARS OLD, my father, who was not a good hustler, presented me with the first serious poem I ever read. Lewis Carroll wrote it in 1845:

> Learn well your grammar and never stammer
> Write well and neatly, and sing most sweetly
> Drink tea, not coffee and never eat toffee
> Eat bread with butter, and once more, don't stutter

In presenting this verse to me, Dad also said that Carroll was a stutterer—but one who had come to find his voice as a writer. My emotionally naïve father thought the poem might offer some levity. Of course, it did no such thing. All it did was confuse me. My stutter itself had been a source of confusion since I'd begun to speak. I didn't understand why my voice, unlike everyone else's, was mysteriously blocked on certain sounds.

The strongest voice of my early life—the one I continue to hear in my head even after his death six years ago at age ninety-five—belonged to my father, Milton Ritz, formidable intellectual and music lover. Dad dug Bach, Bartók, and Stravinsky, and was also wild for jazz. It didn't matter that I was a Charlie Parker modernist and he a Count Basie mainstreamer. His passion was contagious. Enraptured, he'd sit back in an easy chair, close his eyes, and let Mahler transport him. At certain passages, he'd jump up and conduct like Toscanini. After the symphony or song was over, he'd deliver disquisitions on the meaning of it all, contextualizing the historical moment that Mozart wrote his Requiem in D Minor or Duke Ellington wrote his "Black, Brown and Beige."

I was his only son, and he, my main model of what it meant to be a man. Men listen to serious music and read serious books. Men apply critical scrutiny to every aspect of life. Men study philosophy and history. Men understand, as my father never tired of telling me, that the greatest minds of our times were Marx, Freud, and Einstein. These were the men who reshaped our concept of the political, psychological, and material world. Mostly, though, men—effective men, admired men, powerful men—speak with authority and confidence. Like my father, men aren't simply articulate; they are battle-ready verbal warriors who, through the mastery of language, disarm and defeat their opponents at a moment's notice. Their tongues are their swords.

I both admired and feared my father's fluency—admired him as the smartest man I knew, and feared him as someone who, insensitive to my own insecurities, didn't think twice about employing his florid language to put me down. In terms of fierce argumentation, he spoke no differently to me than to his colleagues. That flattered me even as it cowered me.

Beneath his bluster, Dad, the youngest of three brothers, possessed a sweet disposition and a tender heart, but faced heavy frustration. His parents escaped the pogroms in Eastern Europe in the early twentieth century and came to Newark, New Jersey. Their native language was Yiddish and both spoke heavily accented English. Grandpa Hymie repaired radiators. Grandma Lena was a housewife. They were staunch believers in the virtues of the Russian Revolution of 1917. Their loyalty to the Communist Party was absolute, even after the ascendency of Joseph Stalin. Rebelling against his parents, my precocious father became a follower of Leon Trotsky, an original architect of the revolution who, in exile, vehemently opposed Stalin and was eventually assassinated by the Soviet leader's henchmen. To Dad and his high school friends, Trotskyism represented an intellectual radicalism that infuriated my grandparents, especially Hymie, an outspoken leader in Newark's Communist cells.

As a child, my father witnessed his father beaten by police during political rallies. During his teen years, Dad would suffer a similar fate. Yet father and son never bonded. Other than rallying the forces from the podium, Hymie was taciturn and enigmatic. I still see him sitting in an overstuffed easy chair in the cramped apartment he shared with Lena, his head buried in the *Morning Freiheit*, the Yiddish Communist paper. Only occasionally would he look up and smile. In contrast, my father's mother was warm and embracing. I adored her and, in turn, felt adored by her.

There was no adoration between Milton and his folks. They remained estranged for life. Adding to his frustration was the fact that several of his radical high school friends went on to college and spectacularly successful careers. His closest friend, Leslie Fiedler, became a famous literary critic and eventually my graduate school mentor.

In the midst of the Great Depression, there was no money for Dad to go to college. After graduating high school, he scrambled to find work wherever he could. He wound up in the mailroom of a hat factory on Lower Broadway in Manhattan, where my mother (as well as her mother) operated sewing machines. I do believe that my parents fell in love, although rancor and betrayal marked their relationship for decades to come.

Pearl Graver was beautiful, sharp, and practical, the product of a painful upbringing in the slums of the Lower East Side. Milton was all about ideas, art, and radical politics. She was gutsy and unafraid of adventure. As is often the case with bullies, he was essentially fearful. She wanted a new life. He wanted confidence. They joined forces. Where Milton was emotionally weak, Pearl was strong. His intellectual interests intrigued her. Her sensuality attracted him. She felt ashamed that she had left high school before graduation. He reassured her by validating her native intelligence. He had culture. She had street smarts. Occasionally she wandered into Catholic churches, where the silent iconography and pungent incense intrigued her, but, as a Jew, Pearl remained an outsider looking in. Milton's Marxism said no to religion. Just before the start of World War II, they married at City Hall.

Their first child, my sister Esther, was born on Christmas day 1942. I was conceived shortly thereafter because, from what Dad told me, he hoped that two infants would keep him out of the army. My mother said she wanted a second child regardless. Either way, the plan didn't work, and on the day I was born, December 2, 1943, my father was in an army camp in Alabama, training for the infantry. He fell during a climbing exercise and broke his leg. He also broke down emotionally and spent several months in the army hospital. My mother was certain that the fall was his calculated way to avoid battle. Dad denied it. Although his discharge was not labeled dishonorable, the experience traumatized him. The rest of his company was dispatched to the European front and was wiped out to a man. He told me the story when I was a teen, dwelling on the fact that the man in the hospital bed next to him was a celebrated translator of the great Spanish poet Federico García Lorca.

"We discussed everyone from William Faulkner to Fyodor Dostoyevsky," said Dad. "Those conversations brought me back to sanity."

After their marriage, my parents lived in Brooklyn, but we eventually settled in Newark, Dad's home turf, where my younger sister, Elizabeth, was born in 1949. The night classes he had taken in philosophy at the City College of New York didn't lift him out of the working class. He drove a truck, delivering pretzels to local bars. Sometimes he took me along.

One winter Saturday night, when I was nine, my father told me that our next stop would be a jazz club, the Broadway Lounge in downtown Newark. I grew excited. Although I loved the records Dad played at home, I had never heard music performed live. He pulled the truck into an alley, parked, and started lugging out tins of pretzels. I carried a few of the smaller ones. The second we stepped into the club, the music, although sweet and gentle, assaulted me. A haze of smoke covered the rectangular room, where sharply dressed black patrons sat at tables facing a small stage. A drummer, pianist, and bassist were backing a singer whose fragile face looked neither male nor female. He was short as a child but appeared strangely ageless. His voice ached with the pain I associated with Billie Holiday, my parents' favorite singer, whose hypnotically tragic stories I heard as the soundtrack to their troubled marriage. Billie spoke to me with an intimacy I didn't understand but cherished. The intimacy comforted me, the wonder of pain transformed into melody.

Now this new singer did the same.

"It's Little Jimmy Scott," my dad whispered to me. "He lives here in Newark and records for the same label as Charlie Parker."

"So he's a man," I said.

"An angel. Just listen."

Hearing tears in the singer's voice, I asked Dad, "Is he crying?"

"Yes. Angels cry."

A month later, my father took me to a concert. My mother, who suffered with a depression that inexplicably turned to contempt for both my father and me, refused to leave her bedroom. Dad and I went to Newark's Mosque Theater to see Billie Holiday. In contrast to the smoky club where I saw Little Jimmy, this was an ornate concert hall where symphonic orchestras performed. Yet like Jimmy, Billie's only accompanists were a pianist, bassist, and drummer. She was regal: long black dress, long white gloves, her hair artfully arranged on the left side of her noble head and highlighted with a garland of white flowers. She didn't move her arms. She simply stood there and sang, gently nodding to the rhythm that supported her stories of spending mornings welcoming heartache and evenings covering the waterfront. Her heart was broken. My young heart beat madly. I had liked jazz before, but now like turned to love.

Walking to the car after the show, Dad and I happened by the stage door, where a group of photographers gathered to shoot Billie's exit. We stayed to catch a glimpse. We didn't have to wait long. She appeared swathed in white fur and a white-feathered, wide-brimmed black hat. Flashbulbs popped. A journalist shouted out a question.

"Miss Holiday! Miss Holiday! What singers are you listening to these days?"

She stopped and smiled, apparently pleased with the question. When she answered, her voice dripped like honey.

"Oh, a man who lives right here in Newark. Little Jimmy Scott. He's my favorite."

A lifetime later, on the other side of the country, I would meet Jimmy and chronicle his story, which was as complex and heartbreaking as Billie's. But on this cold night in Newark, a million dreams ago, all I knew was that the two singers were connected in sound and soul. And though I was a child who couldn't explain why, I felt part of that connection.

The connection was the seductive allure of voices calling me from a different culture that spoke in a different manner. My own culture, based in the predominantly Weequahic section of the city, was Jewish. The older generation, like my grandparents, spoke Yiddish. My mother spoke a hard, nasal New Yorkese. Dad's speech was loftier. He went off on elaborate verbal riffs that prompted Mom's inevitable intervention: "Milton, stop with the bullshit."

My own speech alarmed my parents, who conscientiously sent me to therapists for much of my childhood. I didn't mind the sessions. I saw that the breathing and relaxation techniques were designed to help me. Yet they didn't. The stutter was stubborn and mystified the many psychologists who tried to temper it. Early on, I realized I had to live with it. The toughest challenge was school. In the early grades, the worst moments came when I was asked to speak my name. We stutterers learn to substitute easy-to-say words for difficult ones, but we can't substitute our names. We're forced to announce ourselves in the most humiliating manner possible, defining our identity in a catastrophe of ineptitude. "What's wrong," one especially insensitive teacher said as I struggled to get past the block, "you don't even know your own name?" The other kids howled.

Rejection and ridicule from my peers were mitigated by acceptance and love from my family. I felt particularly drawn to my mother's side, working-class people who'd survived the crushing intensity of the Lower East Side. They were truck drivers and cabdrivers and laundry operators, gamblers and bookkeepers and seamstresses who were salty and raw and couldn't have cared less about my stutter. Maybe that's because their own relationship to language lacked self-consciousness. They liked fracturing the King's English. They took to me because they saw how I took to them. They were warm and funny and crude and emotional. They sensed that I liked attention, and gave it to me. They saw that I liked dressing sharp, and complimented me on my outlandish bow ties.

While my father and I bonded over books and music and the fact that we were both targets of Pearl Ritz's disdain, my mother and I bonded over clothes. She was a superb seamstress; a whiz at the Singer sewing machine. It doesn't surprise me that, in writing this section of the book, I dreamt of her only last night. I was lost in a vast department store and frightened I'd never find my way out. Suddenly there she was, her arms open. I ran to her; she held me as I wept. I cannot recall an instance when, even as a young boy, I wept in my mother's arms. Her remoteness and inexplicable anger kept us apart emotionally. Her dark moods frightened me, just as they frightened my father.

Shopping, though, brought out a different Pearl. She had style. She knew how to put together an outfit. Because she loved fine clothes and luxurious fabrics, she introduced me to high-end department stores. At Lord & Taylor and Bergdorf Goodman, no matter how dire our finances, she would splurge on me. It was the one area where she could express her love. If I couldn't decide between a beige or baby-blue cashmere sweater, she inevitably said, "Take both." I was thrilled not only by the plush of the cashmere but also by the indulgence of the purchase. She was drawn to luxury as a means to defy our present circumstances, both financial and emotional. She told me the heartbreaking story of how, working at the hat factory where she met my father, she had saved enough money to buy a mink coat from a wholesaler on the Lower East Side, only to have the fur stolen. As she spoke, I felt her anguish.

Money was always a source of tension in our household. As children of the Depression, my parents reacted to our working-class status in different ways. My father was frightened; my mother was not. My mother faced the future with unmitigated courage. For her—and, by extension, for me—beautiful clothes connoted a future filled with possibilities. Beautiful clothes meant that one day I might do beautiful things and that, in fact, I might even be a beautiful person. As my sense of style evolved radically over a lifetime, my fascination with clothes never waned. Today I am more fascinated by fashion than ever. Department stores and boutiques give me a feeling of well-being. I am an intrepid shopper. The shopping experience and the purchase of stylish clothes link me to my mother, a woman whose no-nonsense wisdom about the material world—look good, feel good—I accepted as basic truth.

ANOTHER BASIC TRUTH that I accepted as a preteen was my sexual attraction to boys as well as girls. Surprisingly, I wasn't alarmed. Maybe that's due to the liberal household in which I was raised. My father spoke of homosexual writers—Walt Whitman, Marcel Proust, Federico García Lorca, James Baldwin, Jean Genet—with unrestrained admiration. In his library, I also discovered biologist-sexologist Alfred C. Kinsey's *Sexual Behavior in the Human Male,* where I learned that nearly half of all men have sexual feelings for both genders at some point in their lives. I was both fascinated and relieved. I had far more apprehension about my speech impediment than my bisexuality.

Yet the power of my sexual energy—the passion with which I devoured the novels of D. H. Lawrence and Henry Miller—was alarming. I felt overwhelmed by sex. I often still do.

Early on, I felt how the music I loved was connected to sex, but it wasn't until we left New York that I felt its connection to the sacred.

"YES, JESUS! YES, YES, YES!"

N THE FIFTIES, my father became a salesman of men's hats. We moved from Newark to Charleston, South Carolina, where we lived only a year before finally settling in Dallas, Texas.

Dallas seemed to offer nothing. When we arrived, I saw it as one big, boring suburban sprawl. We lived in a small $15,000 house in a northern section of the city called Walnut Hill, not the more affluent Preston Hollow area that housed the majority of the Jews. My father joined a synagogue, Temple Emanu-El, and developed a friendship with

DAVID RITZ

its progressive rabbi, Levi Olan, whose socialist background was similar to Dad's. I'd listen in on their discussions about the failure of Marxism. A religious leader who understood the ideological differences between Trotsky and Stalin was of comfort to my father.

"I'm not interested in God, but I am interested in secular humanism" was his new mantra. My mother agreed to join Olan's congregation. She liked the idea that her family, in their new Dallas home, would affiliate with a Jewish synagogue.

I agreed to a bar mitzvah. My stammer hadn't diminished, but since much of the service is sung—and I never stutter when singing—I had to worry only about my formal spoken address to the congregation. Still more motivated by gaining attention than paralyzed by fear, I figured I'd get by. And I did. The ceremony was held in a small chapel. We didn't know nearly enough people to fill the main sanctuary. I did fine. Afterward, we had a small reception at our house attended by a few new acquaintances. The experience was notable for what it lacked: spirituality. I still felt no connection to God. I still had no conception of God. I merely went through the paces.

During the year I was preparing for my bar mitzvah, my spiritual connection to jazz intensified. I discovered the nearby Walnut Hill record store, where I bought my first records by Ray Charles. The power of Ray's early 45s—"I Got a Woman," "Losing Hand," "Blackjack," "Drown in My Own Tears"—shook me to my core. It wasn't jazz. It was rhythm and blues, which I understood to be jazz's salty uncle. Like jazz, R & B stimulated me even as it relaxed me, a paradox that felt like paradise.

I needed to hear the music live. I needed to experience its creation in real time. That need drew me into the realm of the Other. Finding jazz in New York was as easy as walking down Fifty-Second Street. In New York and Newark, even as a preteen, I'd heard Miles Davis, Charles Mingus, and Thelonious Monk all within a month. Finding jazz in Dallas, on the other hand, required a ninety-minute bus trip from white North Dallas to black South Dallas, with a transfer in downtown, where the white clerk at a record store didn't know of any jazz clubs. A black custodian, though, overheard my question and wrote out a list of places. "Soon as the sun goes down," he said, "these joints will be jumpin.'"

By eight o'clock, I was seated in one such joint. The jovial proprietor didn't care that I was underage. It was a small club in a strip mall where, at a tiny table in the back, I sipped a Coke and listened to a quartet blowing a funky cool I thought I'd left behind in Manhattan.

"There's an after-church jam session tomorrow at American Woodman Hall just down the street," the club owner advised. "Starts at two p.m. That's when the cats get serious and the music gets to sizzle."

Next day, after repeating the long journey from North Dallas, I was walking to Woodman when I passed by a large church. The music pouring out of the open windows startled me. I stopped in my tracks. After a few seconds, I walked to the front of the building, where the doors were open. Behind the altar was a choir of black women and men in red robes. Their harmonies were lush. Standing before them was a girl with smiling eyes who looked to be my age. Her voice soared over the choir and pierced my heart. I felt myself falling in love. Supporting the enormous sound were an organ, bass, and drums, driving the beat with an unholy ferocity that made me want to dance. The congregants, some forty strong, were shouting at the singers, crying, "Yes, Jesus! Yes, yes, yes!"

I wanted to shout along with them. I wanted to walk inside the church. I wanted to walk inside the music. And when the preacher, a compact, broad-shouldered man packed into a coral-blue sharkskin suit, started asking, "Are you ready? Are you ready to receive him? Are you ready to surrender to his grace, his power, his healing love?" I wanted to shout back, "Yes, Jesus! Yes, yes, yes!"

Instead, I said nothing. I remained on the street. I stayed still. I was the outsider looking in. Despite the fact that every fiber of my being wanted to surrender to the celebration, despite the warmth and joy of the magnetic energy inside that church, I couldn't take the step. I couldn't say yes to something I didn't know or understand, something that wasn't part of my culture or history.

An older woman sitting in the last pew noticed me standing at the door. She got up and approached, a broad smile on her face.

"Come in," she said. "You're welcome here. What's your name?"

I tried to say "David," but the word stuck in my throat. I couldn't get it out.

"Don't make no difference," she said. "Jesus knows your name. Jesus knows you."

He does? I asked myself.

Baffled and uncertain, I thanked the woman but walked away.

Why? Unlike my bar mitzvah and the boring hours I spent at Temple Emanu-El confirmation class, there was nothing perfunctory about this experience. It was visceral, thrilling, nearly irresistible. *Nearly.* My heart was screaming yes, but my head was screaming no. The pressures were too great. I couldn't face my family or the Jewish society that we had recently embraced. Instead, I processed it as an adventure into a foreign culture. To protect myself from the pull of Christ—a pull that lasted six long decades—I learned to view myself as an ethnomusicologist fascinated by a culture I could only observe but whose membership was off-limits.

My father, whose intellect intimidated and consoled me, reinforced that attitude. When I told him about the church experience, he had a ready reply. "You were moved by the music," he said. "That's all there is to it."

"But there *was* more to it," I insisted.

"Of course there was. There was sexual suppression. That's what makes it so explosive. Unexpressed sexual energy channeled into artistic extravagance. It's beautiful, but it has nothing to do with Jesus or God or any of the man-made myths created to allay our fears."

Sexual suppression. Unexpressed sexual energy.

I was flattered that my father spoke to me as a peer, but I was uneasy discussing sex. My flattery, of course, was misplaced. Dad didn't see me as a peer. In discussions with his adolescent son, he simply lacked sensitivity and discretion—which was why, only months later, he took me into his confidence to confess his extramarital affair. He went into detail about how his lover allowed sexual acts that my mother would not. As he spoke, I cringed. But I was nonetheless fascinated and felt myself being brought into a tighter bond with my father. I didn't realize he was using me to assuage his guilt. All I knew was that he had shared, with me and me alone, a potent and dangerous secret. "A secret," he said, "that you must never reveal."

Because I kept that secret, I became his coconspirator, sharing his shame and feeling that I, too, was cheating on my mother. Part of that cheating felt like revenge for Mom's inexplicable rage toward me.

"She sees you as the father who left her," said Dad. "She even named you after him. He, too, was David. Jewish people never name their children after the living, but your mother insisted. It was her way of killing him off. Her anger has everything to do with him and nothing to do with you. Don't take it personally."

His words confused rather than comforted me. Part of the confusion was that, despite the animosity between my parents, they were extraordinarily close. All my life, I saw them at the kitchen table: my mother smoking cigarettes and drinking black coffee, my father deep in thought, discussing for hours on end their troubled relationship and the problems of their children. They were not only passionately committed to our welfare, but also couldn't stop talking about us. They were at their best when we fell into crisis, always there to help, whether successfully or not. Their own marital crisis was an ongoing phenomenon, and though they dissected it ad nauseam, I knew that my father did so dishonestly. His secret lover remained secret.

Yet I continued to look up to him and compare my skills with his. He read more than me. He knew more than me. He spoke better than me. In particular, it was his lofty language, rendered without hesitancy or impairment, that left me deflated.

When it came to music, though, my deflation about being in Dallas was short-lived. I found several other black churches that featured full-throated singers and booming choirs. Rather than stay outside, I screwed up my courage and sat in a back pew. I also became fascinated with several preachers whose dramatic sermons mirrored the music. It wasn't the content that moved me but rather their rhetorical flourishes, the way their preaching, like a jazzman's solo, was geared to please the ear and stir the heart while retaining a natural conversational flow.

I was deeply moved by shows at the Sportatorium, a huge barn of an arena that held wrestling matches, a country music radio show called the *Big D Jamboree*, and occasional performances by black gospel groups. I attended the gospel concerts religiously. At the time, I had no idea that I was witnessing the last great expression of the golden age of gospel, a time when vocal groups, both male and female, had perfected the art of close-knit harmony, infusing sacred song with overt sensuality. There were the Caravans, the Davis Sisters, Clara Ward and the Famous Ward Sisters, the Staple Singers, the Sensational Nightingales, the Dixie Hummingbirds, the original Blind Boys of Alabama, the Mighty Clouds of Joy, the Swan Silvertones. The poetry of their names, like the openhearted poetry of Walt Whitman, whom I had recently discovered, fired my imagination. Their music fractured me. I thought I knew what greatness in black music was all about: Ben Webster and Duke Ellington, Lester Young and Billie Holiday, Dizzy Gillespie and Charlie Parker. But this music was equally great, as emotional, complex, and compelling. Just as compelling was the presentation. The female singers were decked out in flowing robes and fabulous hairdos; the men wore color-coordinated suits of lime green and Popsicle orange.

The musical glory reached its pinnacle in the person of Sam Cooke, then lead singer with the Soul Stirrers. I saw him at the Sportatorium in 1956, the same year that Elvis Presley made a splash with "Blue Suede Shoes." Listening to a friend's copy of the first Elvis album, I wasn't impressed. Elvis sang Ray Charles's "I Got a Woman" with far less fervor than Ray. I saw pictures of teenage girls screaming at Elvis's shows and wondered why. At the Soul Stirrers' show, though, I saw why Sam Cooke had his way with women. When Sam sang "Touch the Hem of His Garment," referring to a healing narrated in the Gospels, females, young and old, reached out to touch Sam's hem—or whatever part of his body they could reach. You could taste the sugar in his voice, the salt, the honey, the cream. He left the worshippers spent. Women wept; men fell into trances; the Holy Ghost washed over the congregation like a tidal wave.

My dad wouldn't accompany me to the gospel events. He said all that Jesus business would make him uncomfortable, but he did agree to go with me to hear live jazz. This happened when the men's hat industry was in a downward spiral, and he sought relief from the grind of his time on the road. Business was so bad, in fact, that in order to make the mortgage, my mother worked the night shift assembly line at Texas Instruments.

Rather than ride the bus, I was happy to have Dad drive us to American Woodman Hall. The room held some three hundred people and housed a jazz session that had become my Sunday ritual. Admission was a dollar. You sat at one of the dozens of long tables covered with white paper tablecloths. It was smoky and crowded and celebratory. The patrons were exclusively black, an after-church congregation of party people dressed to kill—men in supersharp suits of pin-striped purple and banana yellow, women in form-fitting sequined dresses and dazzling earrings. You brought your own bottles of booze and bought buckets of ice and soft drinks. A basket of chicken and fries cost a dollar.

The music was a mix of the Miles Davis–informed modern jazz and soul-heavy sounds of Ray Charles. The house band was the Red Tops, and some of the players, including David "Fathead" Newman and James Clay—the two men who later significantly impacted my professional life—already had national reputations. The music was good enough to please my critical father. He was fascinated by the place and said he felt at home. He approached the promoter/master of ceremonies, Tony Davis—a grizzly bear of a man who wore a black patch over one eye—to compliment him on his green felt fedora.

"I think you'd like a new stingy-brim model that just came out," Dad said.

During the next break in the music, the two men walked to the parking lot, where Dad opened the sample case that he carried in the trunk of his car. Tony bought a half dozen hats, cash on the barrelhead.

As the hat business declined, Dad's only steady buyers were stores in black neighborhoods. In one such establishment in Houston, he encountered the Queen of the Blues, Dinah Washington, who, along with Billie Holiday, Ella Fitzgerald, and Sarah Vaughan, drove me wild. He brought me Dinah's autograph, "To David, a big fan with a big love of the music," that I framed and hung on the wall next to photos of Nat King Cole and John Coltrane. Soon every inch of my bedroom was covered with images of the giants of jazz who, in my mind, were the unmet friends leading me through the labyrinth of adolescence. In the sixties, I hung up a photograph of a new singer on the scene who already seemed to belong in the pantheon of greats. His name was Marvin Gaye.

SEXUAL
HEALING

USED THE SUCCESS OF *BROTHER RAY* to chase after Marvin Gaye. Meeting Marvin represented a critical moment in both my personal and professional lives. "Sexual Healing," the song we wrote together, though thought to be essentially sensuous, was far more than that. The song had a decidedly spiritual component.

There was always something sacred about Marvin's voice. I heard it when I was smitten by his early hits. Beneath the silky smooth delivery in songs such as "I Heard It Through the Grapevine," I felt that he was praying. That feeling was confirmed when he released the openly Christian *What's Going On* in 1971, only to be followed two years later by the wildly erotic *Let's Get It On.*

We met after the critics had slammed 1978's *Here, My Dear,* Marvin's idiosyncratic suite of songs dedicated to his first wife, Anna Gordy Gaye, that detailed their ruinous relationship. I rebutted the *LA Times*'s harsh review in a letter to the editor. I called the double album a masterpiece comparable to the best work of Duke Ellington and Stevie Wonder. The song titles were striking: "When Did You Stop Loving Me, When Did I Stop Loving You," "Anger," "You Can Leave, But It's Going to Cost You." Even the artwork, an illustration depicting symbols of pain and divorce dominated by Marvin clad in a toga and posing as a Roman senator, was singular. My aim in praising the record was twofold: I wanted to defend Marvin, but I also hoped he'd see what I wrote and reach out to me. He did just that.

We became fast friends. Marvin had just read *Brother Ray* and decided he wanted to tell his own story. I was thrilled. The experience with Ray was beautiful, yet always a little scary. Ray was a taskmaster, a strict uncle. Marvin was a cool older brother. At thirty-nine, he was four years my senior. He divided his time between his private recording studio on Sunset Boulevard and the home he had purchased for his parents in the Crenshaw district, just two miles from where I lived with Roberta, Alison, and Jessica.

Our first meeting took place in his studio. When I walked in, Marvin was seated behind the engineering board, leaning into a microphone and composing a song. The act was pure improvisation. Even though his vocal was amplified through enormous speakers, it remained restrained. Inside his voice, I heard that familiar tear. But being in his presence, I also felt an urgency that hadn't registered on his records. As he sang, his eyes closed. He addressed a woman, urging her to "let your love come shining through." But the focus soon changed. The sudden shift was to a song of praise: praise God when you work, praise God when you play, praise him when you're sad, praise him when you're glad, praise him when you dance, when you make romance, praise him every day in every way. Marvin was, in fact, praying.

When the song was finished, he half opened his eyes and saw me. His smile was soft. His speaking voice was equally soft. He thanked me for my defense of *Here, My Dear* and asked if, before we began to chat, I'd mind if he continued working for a while. If that meant listening to Marvin sing, I hoped that he'd work for hours. And he did.

Before he began, he lit a joint and passed it my way.

"You smoke?" he asked.

"Yes."

I took a hit and settled back into the deep cushions of the couch.

The high was strong. Not surprisingly, I started tripping:

I was in Marvin Gaye's studio watching him invent songs on the spot. I was also mesmerized by Marvin's grooves, grooves that I wanted to go on forever because, as long as they pulsated, all was right with the world. These gentle grooves, whether created by pianist Fats Waller or clarinetist Edmond Hall, had been calming me down while also revving me up ever since I was a child.

When he took a break, I expressed that idea to him.

"Interesting," he said in a mellow tone. "Jesus put it this way: 'You must come to me as a child.'"

I wasn't expecting that response. And I wasn't sure what to say.

"It's the Gospel of Mark," Marvin continued. "'Truly, I say to you, whoever does not receive the Kingdom of God like a child shall not enter it.' The Lord knew that before the world gets hold of children, they're pure. It pains me to reflect on my loss of purity. When I sing, it's purity I pray for because purity lives on the other side of pain."

He closed his eyes, breathed deeply, and said, "I'm a Christian, or at least try to be. When I fail, which is often, it's because I block myself from God's love. I sin. Everyone does, but my definition of sin is very specific."

"What is it?" I asked.

"Sin is when we separate ourselves from God."

"Are you sinning, then, when you create secular music?"

"Not at all. That's an old myth; a leftover superstition from my father's generation that said keep the devil's music out of church. Singing about sex doesn't exclude the presence of sacred spirit. Or does it? Who has the key to marry spirit to flesh? Once I thought I possessed it, but in reality I lost it long ago."

"How?"

"I lost it in the morass of show business. I lost it in a sea of self-centeredness."

Marvin's musings, even when self-critical, were tinged with humor. His aura was light, his demeanor sweet. His half-sloped eyes conveyed gentleness. His speech had the effortless flow of his music.

"If you think it's the pot triggering these thoughts, you're wrong," he said. "All weed does is give me a slight out-of-body experience so I can see myself from a distance."

"And what do you see?" I asked.

"A dude high on weed."

Marvin lived high. Steady smoking and frequent coking were daily rituals. He also organized weekly basketball games at the Hollywood YMCA near his studio and, once every few months, went on organic cleansing programs and stopped doping.

I had long loved pot, which brought me closer to the music and musicians I revered. Cocaine put me on edge, but

I found the edge exciting. When Marvin offered to share his drugs, I had no inclination to refuse. I wanted to gain entrance into his world of exotic highs.

Marvin had separated from his second wife, Janis, who was seventeen years his junior. (First wife Anna, an older sister of Motown Records founder Berry Gordy, was seventeen years his senior.) He was at his parents' home, where he invited me to a prayer meeting with his mother, Alberta, his older sister, Jeanne, and his younger brother, Frankie. We sat around the kitchen table in the roomy old home and joined hands. Noticeably absent was his minister father, who was secluded in his upstairs bedroom.

"When two or more are gathered in his name," said Marvin, "Jesus is among us, in this kitchen, in our hearts. Today and every day, may our path be directed by his loving light."

He spoke about seeing Jesus in everyone.

"When you're encountering kindness, you're encountering Jesus," he said. "When you're looking at compassion, you're looking at him."

In the afternoon, we began discussing our fathers and our difficulties relating to them.

"I think it's time we call them up and tell them that we love them," I suggested.

Marvin agreed.

I called my dad in Dallas and spoke the words.

Marvin's turn. All he had to do was go upstairs, where his father was reading the Bible in his bedroom.

"I can't," he said.

"Why not?" I asked.

His shut his eyes and let out a long sigh. "Just because I can't."

MARVIN AND I set out on our literary collaboration. I spent months in his studio; I went on the road with him; we visited his childhood neighborhood in Washington, DC. His candor never faltered, even as his circumstances worsened: the IRS, after him for back taxes, took possession of his studio. Motown, his home label for decades, was hounding him for a long-overdue album. Anna and Jan were suing him for unpaid child support. On the brink of bankruptcy, he fled to Hawaii, living in a bread van on the beach, and then to London, where freebase cocaine ravaged his mind. Out of both concern and cunning, a concert promoter brought him to Ostend, Belgium. It was there, during a harsh winter, that Marvin struggled to regain his footing.

Though we had spoken by phone several times, it wasn't until the spring of 1982 that Marvin invited me to Ostend. The streets were clean, the air clear and cold, the wind bracing. I saw the city as an oasis of bourgeois European charm. Well-dressed locals strolled the seaside promenade with their poodles and Pekingese; the restaurants and taverns served up platters of fresh flounder and shrimp; the pace of urban life was, as Marvin put it, "a beat back from London or New York."

Marvin's apartment overlooked the vast North Sea. We usually met there at night when the water was lit by moonlight and the sky crowded with stars. His front room afforded a full view of the cruise ships, tankers, and tugboats floating by.

Marvin looked exhausted. He had gained weight around the middle. His puffy eyes said he had been through hell. But he said he was back. He'd made it through and was ready to forge ahead. He'd quit Motown and signed with Columbia Records, for which he was determined to deliver a debut smash. He wanted to punctuate his prolonged European exile with a hit record.

We went back to work on the book, but also jogged on the beach and walked through the woods outside the city. We sat in ancient churches and played darts in the bars. Late one night, alone in his apartment, we watched a documentary on John Coltrane. The title of Coltrane's most spiritual composition, *A Love Supreme*, moved Marvin deeply. He viewed that supreme love as Jesus and began discussing his miracles. He pointed to the Book of Mark, chapter 1, lines 140 to 145, where a leper comes to the Lord and asks if he is willing to cleanse him.

"I can see Jesus stretching out his hand and touching the man," said Marvin, "while gently whispering 'Be cleansed.'"

Marvin closed his eyes and stayed silent. Several long seconds passed before he began speaking of his father. There was the joy of his father's Spirit-filled storefront church, but there was also the violence Marvin endured at the hands of a man who, before beating him, forced him to strip. This was the same father, the same charismatic preacher, who deeply confused his family by donning women's wigs, blouses, and undergarments.

"Did the beatings and cross-dressing make you doubt his theology?" I asked.

"I remember the beauty of his sermons. The beauty of his singing voice. I remember the church saints, the women in white shouting the holy name of Jesus, the women embracing me, bringing me close to their bosoms, keeping me safe in the bosom of the Lord. We change. We waver. But Jesus remains constant. His love is unbreakable. I felt that love from the beginning. It wasn't anything I learned. It was something I felt. I still do. I still believe."

As we spoke, a cassette played on a boom box. The music throbbed with a reggae-like rhythm. There were no lyrics or melody. Marvin was certain that this track, written by his keyboardist, Odell Brown, had the makings of a hit, but he lacked a story. The second the tape stopped, he rewound it and played it from the top. I felt the groove infectiously fueling our conversation.

Marvin continued to speak on the goodness of the Lord. He explained that the ultimate manifestation of an inaudible and invisible God was the fleshly Jesus, who, both human and divine, expressed the loving nature of his Creator.

Given the sweet nature of Marvin's music, I saw how the artist and his art were forged by faith. It was then that I noticed a book sitting on the coffee table: an elaborately bound volume of cartoon illustrations by Georges Pichard, a Frenchman, Marvin explained, who applied an avant-garde sensibility to kinky sex.

"Take a look," he urged.

I was taken aback. The drawings depicted women being sexually brutalized. Seeing my shock, Marvin began quoting the Marquis de Sade.

" 'Sex is as important as eating or drinking,' he wrote, 'and we ought to allow the one appetite to be satisfied with as little restraint or false modesty as the other.' "

"But the infliction of vicious pain . . ." I protested.

"It is only by way of pain," Marvin continued, paraphrasing the marquis, "that one arrives at pleasure."

"And you find these drawings compatible with the teachings of Christ?"

"Christ resolved the war of the spirit and the flesh. I have not."

"But don't you want to stop the war? Don't you want to heal the pain?"

He answered my question with one of his own: "Sex is never a painful subject for you?"

I told him that, as long as I could remember, I was sexually attracted to both genders. I was married to Roberta, a woman I loved deeply, but no matter how satisfying our physical relationship, my homosexual side had not abated.

Marvin spoke of his own sexual complexity. He confessed that, like his father, he liked adorning himself in women's clothing.

"My father isn't gay," he said, "but his feminine sensibility is strong. Mine as well. With that comes shame. Does bisexuality cause pain in you?"

"Only in that I can't always have what I want."

I went on to explain that, at my urging, Roberta had agreed to an open marriage earlier in the seventies that proved disastrous and resulted in confusion, jealousy, and uncertainty.

"I understand," said Marvin as he rewound the music track and started it from the beginning. A minute ticked by before I said, "Sexual healing."

Marvin broke out into a broad smile.

"What's that?" he asked.

"Sexual healing is something that's good for you," I said. "The pain is healed, and there's no need to keep pursuing it."

"That might be the story I've been looking for. Write it out. Let it flow."

On a yellow pad, I wrote, "Whenever blue tears are falling and my emotional stability is leaving me, there is something I can do . . ."

In a matter of minutes, I wrote the rest of the words, culminating with "Sexual healing is something that's good for me." Marvin took the words and, as if each syllable were attached to a musical note, fashioned a melody. In less than a half hour, the song was written.

I had ghostwritten a book before, and now, I saw, I could ghostwrite a song. I could channel the anguish that I felt in Marvin's heart and give it poetic form. In that sense, I thought the song was about Marvin. I was right, but I was also wrong. It would take years for me to learn that the song was about me.

MARVIN'S BELIEF IN JESUS was unwavering. When what would be his final album, *Midnight Love*, was released in 1982, the last two items in his acknowledgments were to "thank David Ritz, whose brilliant literary mind created the title 'Sexual Healing'" and to proclaim, "I still love Jesus, all praises to the Heavenly Father."

I was moved by the latter comment and perplexed by the former.

I was moved because, although Marvin was back on crack and in a downward spiral that would lead to his demise, he never doubted the love ethos of Jesus. His faith was strong, but his theological rationale ruinous. He came to reason that the devil, not God, was winning the global war for the heart of mankind. In 1981 he'd titled his penultimate album *In Our Lifetime?* because he was convinced the end of the world was at hand. No matter how fiercely he had rejected his father, he couldn't shed Marvin Pentz Gaye Sr.'s Pentecostal indoctrination. These were the last days. So why not just give in to the devil and party? That meant more drugs, more madness, and more fury at his father, the same fury that, I believe, led to Marvin's self-willed destruction.

The mention of me on the back of the album came as a shock. I had expected to see my name listed under the title of "Sexual Healing," along with Odell Brown, who had written the chords and rhythm track, and Marvin, who had written the melody.

Naturally, I loved the compliment, but what about the actual credit? Marvin had assured me that my name would be on the song. In fact, in the taped conversation I had made during the session—I taped all my interviews with Marvin— he had said that I'd helped him write a smash hit.

I had no reason not to trust him. At that point, we'd spent dozens of hours together discussing everything. "If I tell it to you honestly," Marvin said, "I know you'll write it honestly." His love-hate relationship with Berry Gordy; his fear of having inherited his father's penchant for cross-dressing; his nearly crippling performance anxiety (both as a singer and a lover); his attempts to shore up his masculinity through boxing, basketball, and, in one famous episode, trying out for the Detroit Lions professional football team—he spoke of it all with astounding candor. He was self-aware, self-critical, and incorrigibly self-involved. He was a master at creating drama laced with biting irony.

Before I left Belgium in the spring of 1982, Marvin told me that he had no intention of ever leaving Europe. He foresaw that coming home would probably do him in. "I'm safe here," he said. "The vast and cold ocean between me and my father gives me peace. The distance protects me."

The cause of Marvin's return to America was not his father, but his mother, with whom he was unnaturally close. She was to undergo a risky operation, and he had to be by her side. So in November 1982, drinking enough champagne to dull his fear of flying, he ended his exile. Only when he

arrived in LA did he learn that his father, despite his wife's ill-
ness, had left the home that Marvin had bought them in LA
and moved back to Washington, DC. That both relieved and
angered him. He was glad not to encounter his father but infuriated that Reverend Gaye, who, under mysterious circumstances, had been ousted from his esoteric church decades
earlier, had deserted his wife at such a critical moment.

Marvin and I spoke on the phone several times, and the
vibe was still positive. With "Sexual Healing" climbing the
charts—his first hit single in nearly six years—he expressed
ongoing gratitude for my contribution. I thanked him for his
warm acknowledgment of me on the back of the album but
said I was concerned that my name didn't appear as a co-
writer and that, as he knew, I created more than just the title.
He agreed.

"That was just an oversight," he said. "You'll be paid."

I took Marvin at his word. I celebrated with him when
Mother Gaye's operation was successful and spent time back
at her home on Gramercy Place for prayer meetings and
meals. Another happy occasion was the birth of April Gay,
daughter to Irene and Frankie, Marvin's younger brother,
who had also become my good friend. Marvin and I went
to the hospital together to see the infant. By then, "Sexual
Healing" had become an international sensation. Marvin
complained that, due to pressure from the IRS for back

taxes, he was still broke, and, to stay solvent, he needed to tour, an obligation he found odious.

Marvin was a recording artist in the purest sense: he was happiest in a closed environment in which every aspect of his music could be manicured. Control mitigated his insecurity. Live performance was a nightmare. Bizarre as it sounds, he worried about his singing ability. His ever-growing paranoia had him convinced that during any given concert, his vocal inadequacy would be exposed.

I mentioned gently that I'd yet to receive credit or money for "Sexual Healing."

"David," he snapped, "stop bothering me about that."

In the five years of our friendship, that was the first time he had ever spoken to me harshly. It shook me up. I let a few weeks go by. I called the woman acting as Marvin's manager, but she played dumb. Other inquiries got me nowhere. Finally, I asked the advice of Jerry Wexler, a hardened music biz pro, who had worked with Ray Charles and served as Aretha Franklin's main producer.

"Sue him!" he screamed over the phone.

"But Jerry, this is Marvin, my friend, my—"

"Sue him!" he shouted again. "If you don't, you'll wind up without a dime. This is the music business, where friendship counts for nothing."

At a time when my own finances were on shaky ground—

we were basically living on Roberta's salary—Jerry's words hit home. At the same time, I figured I owed Marvin one more chance.

The last time we met was at his parents' home on Gramercy Place. The get-together took place in the den-like structure, detached from the main house, where he liked to party. He was wearing an eggshell-blue shirt, a gray herringbone sport coat, and black flannel trousers.

"This is my Cary Grant outfit," said Marvin. "What do you think?"

"Looks like you just graduated Harvard," I answered.

He offered me a hit of his joint and a line of coke. I accepted both. He looked worried and worn out. He said he dreaded the upcoming tour. Our mutual friend Dave Simmons and Marvin's brother, Frankie, were also there. They were joining the tour as security.

Toward the end of the evening, I mentioned once again the matter of credit and money.

"You've gotten your credit," Marvin said. "Your name's on my liner notes. I didn't have to do that, but I did."

Marvin was uptight, his relaxed demeanor gone. His eyes appeared darker. I felt his fear. I also knew there was no arguing with him. I clearly would be getting nothing for the song. But could I really bring a lawsuit? I thought back to those times, especially the prayer meetings, when Marvin and his mom had spoken to me of Jesus. Those were among the most meaningful moments of my adult life. They were not theological disquisitions or heavy-handed interpretations of Scripture. He and Mother Gaye simply sat there and spoke of allowing more love to enter their hearts. Their eyes closed, they allowed great silences punctuated by simple phrases uttered in their softer-than-soft voices: "Love Jesus. Jesus Love. The Lord is love. Just love, sweet love." They prayed for me—not for my salvation or my conversion, but for my willingness to allow God into my life. In those days, before Marvin was freebasing cocaine, his gentleness was remarkable. So was his mother's. Her voice revealed a peace I experienced as sacred. We held hands until Marvin or Mother Gaye would say "Praise his holy name" or "He is here with us now," or Marvin would sing out "Thank you, Jesus!"

The name Jesus, as sung in the songs I had loved so dearly as a child and learned to love even more as an adult, resonated with such strength that I sometimes felt frightened. I used my father's reasoning to explain it away: it was just the music. The music was emotional. Just because the music moved me didn't mean some Holy Spirit had inspired or created it. But what if the music was a true expression of Jesus? Did I have the strength to tell my wife, my parents, and my friends that I, a Jew raised in a secular brand of intellectual Judaism, was embracing Jesus? No.

Further reinforcing my rejection of Jesus was Marvin's fall from grace. He was cheating me. He was also slowly losing his mind. The return of his father to the Gramercy Place home only exacerbated the dilemma. Marvin was trapped inside the Oedipal triangle that had imprisoned him since childhood. Upstairs in that rambling house in midcity LA, his mother slept in one bedroom, his father in another, and Marvin in a third.

I spoke to Jerry Wexler again.

"I love this man," I said. "Deep down, he's the sweetest soul I've ever met."

"Great," said Jerry. "Love him all you want. But business is business. Sue him!"

DIVIDED
SOUL

INITIATED A LAWSUIT. Marvin was served just before going onstage for a "Sexual Healing" concert. That long tour, Marvin's last, was described to me by eyewitnesses, including his ex-wife Jan—with whom I later collaborated on a memoir—as absolute hell. Freebase cocaine fueled his paranoia to psychotic proportions. Every night, he was petrified; every night, he grew increasingly erratic. He was certain someone was out to kill him. While performing, he placed security guards onstage to his left and right. He had his brother, Frankie, and our friend Dave Simmons, both of whom uncannily resembled Marvin, walk beside him wherever he went. He figured the killer would be confused and wouldn't know which Marvin Gaye to shoot. At hotels, he stayed in penthouse suites with three bedrooms. One bedroom was his; in the second, he placed a preacher; in the third, a dope dealer. All night, he ran from one room to another. When, at Marvin's request, Jan joined the tour in Miami, he became violent, and she had to flee his room, fearing for her life. In Baltimore, comic Dick Gregory convinced him to cancel the tour. Dick had a rehabilitation plan for Marvin that required checking into a private facility. Marvin agreed, but when Gregory arrived the next day to whisk Marvin away, the singer was gone and the tour was still on.

The finale of each show was "Sexual Healing," during which Marvin dropped the bathrobe he was wearing and stood before the microphone in black briefs. When it was gently suggested that, because his body was not in the best shape, he might avoid disrobing, Marvin replied, "I have no choice. In their eyes, I'm a sex god and must appear as such. Like all the gods, those who claim to be my worshippers will devour me. I'm doomed."

When the long tour finally ran out of steam, and Marvin came home to Gramercy Place, he was a wreck. The freebasing got worse. He watched pornography for days on end. He entertained prostitutes in the family home. Sitting in the backseat of a car as it drove through the Crenshaw district, he tried jumping out the door, but friends held him back. He was suicidal.

His encounters with his father were brief. During one, he gave Gaye Sr. a pistol. His father asked why. "To protect me," said Marvin. "Assassins are hiding in the bushes."

On April 1, 1984, his dad, high on whiskey, berated his wife for misplacing an insurance form. At the time, Mother Gaye was in Marvin's bedroom, trying to assuage her son's extreme paranoia. High on coke, Marvin warned his dad never to speak harshly to his mother. Gaye Sr. paid no mind and continued chastising his wife. Infuriated, Marvin physically attacked his father, who for decades had warned his son, "I brought you into the world. Lay a hand on me, and I'll take you out."

With that in mind, the father went to his bedroom and returned to face his son. This time the father was holding the .38-caliber revolver his son had given him. He shot Marvin in the chest—twice. Fearing for her own life, Mother Gaye screamed for mercy, begging her husband not to kill her. Her husband had no such intention. He went outside and sat on the front porch, waiting for the police to arrive. He surrendered without incident. At 1:01 p.m. at the California Hospital Medical Center, Marvin was declared dead.

A month later, a tumor was removed from Gaye Sr.'s brain. A judge ruled him competent to stand trial. He pleaded self-defense and ultimately accepted a no-contest agreement that reduced the charge to voluntary manslaughter. Ultimately he was sentenced to five years' probation, avoiding prison. When I visited him, he was cordial and direct. "I did not murder Marvin," he told me. "I wasn't even there that day."

His mind had erased a memory he could not tolerate.

In the aftermath of Marvin's death, my mind reeled. My first feelings were of tremendous grief. The world had lost a singular artist. I had lost a friend. Given our association, I was asked to give dozens of interviews. I refused most of them, but when I did discuss him, I focused on the enduring beauty of his music. Eventually I decided that the book on which we had been collaborating, an autobiography, would have to be scrapped. But given my dozens of hours of interviews with Marvin, I felt both motivated and obligated to write his biography. When I approached his mother, she encouraged me. "You knew him," she said. "Others who didn't will write books about a man whose mind they'll never understand."

Marvin's mind. Did I really understand it? Unlike Ray Charles, who was straight-ahead and flush with confidence, Marvin was overwrought with insecurities. Ray sought pleasure. Marvin not only sought pain but also used his creativity to plot painful scenarios. To punish himself, he had perversely urged both wives to take lovers. He used the resultant agony to inform his art, transforming anxiety into aching beauty.

His dealings with his father were the culmination of his penchant for self-created drama, this one having begun in childhood. The vitriol between the two men, with Mother Gaye in the middle, grew exponentially over the years. Marvin urged his mom to leave the man who had beaten him as a boy, but she never would. Not only did he want his parents divorced, he wanted his father punished. When drugs had diseased his mind, Marvin saw suicide as the only way out. He had tried but failed to do himself in. So, in attacking his father, he achieved what he himself was incapable of achieving: his own exit from a world driving him mad. He also realized two of his other goals: Mother could no longer tolerate her husband and did, in fact, cut off all contact with him; and, according to the tenets of a fundamental theology that Marvin could never quite abandon, Father, a murderer, would be punished for all eternity.

A month after Marvin's death, I sat down and wrote his biography. I quickly found a groove—a rhythm, I hope, that reflected Marvin's rhythms—and completed the book in two months. Much of the time, I was high on pot (which meant a great deal of rewriting the next day). I avoided cocaine except on the day I wrote the words "The End." That evening, a close friend of Marvin's, who had served as his personal photographer, came to my home. I told him that one of his photographs would be on the cover, for which he would be paid. In appreciation, he brought out the pipe and gave me my first hit of freebase cocaine. At the time, my wife and young daughters were asleep upstairs. The high was beyond anything I had experienced. I wanted to climb on the roof and shout the good news to the neighbors. The very next day, I phoned the photographer to thank him but was really calling to ask for more. He didn't return my call. Two days later, I learned that the very night he had left my house, he had been murdered. Rumors said it was over a drug deal gone bad. I never again touched cocaine in any form.

Divided Soul: The Life of Marvin Gaye was published in 1985 to mostly favorable reviews. The book sold well. My father, who looked down on my role as a ghostwriter, was impressed that I had written an independent and (in his mind) literary biography. Now he urged me to continue down this more prestigious path.

He came to visit me in Los Angeles, where I took him to see Etta James, whom he adored, at a small nightclub. After she had sung her signature, "At Last," he said coyly, "Isn't it at last time for you to take your work seriously?"

"What do you mean? I take it dead seriously."

"*Divided Soul* is the breakthrough you've been waiting for. Now it's time to give up the ghost and become a real writer."

"What's real?"

"Your own voice. Your own books. Your own reputation. If James Boswell could write the definitive biography of Samuel Johnson, you can write the definitive biography of Miles Davis."

"If I were to work with Miles," I said, "I'd rather it'd be his book than mine."

"Why in hell would you say that?"

"Because I mean it. Ghosting is fun."

I'm not sure my father looked at literature—or literary work—as fun. He wanted for me what he wanted for himself: literary distinction. Yet it was my father who first explained the concept of ghostwriting to me when I was twelve years old, when he gave me *Lady Sings the Blues* by Billie Holiday (with William Dufty).

"It's beautiful," I said. "It's like she's talking to you. She's really a good writer."

"She didn't write it," said Dad.

"Who did?"

"A man."

"No, she wrote it. She's telling the story."

"She was interviewed by a ghostwriter, William Dufty, who then wrote in her voice."

"Did he get to go over to her house to do the interviews?" I asked.

"I imagine so."

"That sounds like a great job."

"A better job," said Dad, "is to write your own book rather than write a book for someone else. That's true authorship. Ghostwriting is a subgenre."

"What does that mean?"

"You're playing in the minor leagues, not the majors."

"Playing in the minors would be okay if I got to go over to Billie Holiday's house."

FOR MY PART, I was happy with *Divided Soul* because it reflected my deepest understanding of Marvin. The divisions that tore him apart—a love for God, a weakness for demonic intrigue—could never be reconciled.

I also took the book personally. How could I reconcile my own contradictions? In writing a story in which drugs played so negative a role, how could I continue to use drugs to fuel my creative energy? Marvin did so, for sure. But where did it get him? I knew the answer. I wrote the answer. The answer was premature and tragic death. So what was *my* answer? Why did I keep getting high on weed? The answer—that I was addicted—was something I denied. My denial said, *I've written a good book, I haven't lost control, I can manage this thing.* And for years, I did. Or at least thought I did.

My rationalizations were many. I once interviewed bassist Charles Mingus, a mighty force in modern jazz who miraculously married a ferocious avant-garde sensibility to bloodstained gospel grit. When we discussed drugs, he said, "Stick with weed, and you'll be all right. Mellow weed is all you need." Paradoxically, Mingus was the least mellow of all men, a rageaholic who ranted his way through life, but I wanted to believe him, and I did. The truth is that marijuana did not mellow me. It overstimulated me. And paradoxically, it anesthetized me from certain fears while at the same time introducing a subtle level of paranoia to my thinking.

I further rationalized that, given the success of *Divided Soul*, for which I wrote the initial draft under the influence, how bad could the substance be? My friend and mentor Jerry Wexler, who smoked grass into his seventies, called it the "good herb." I saw it as a friend. If only Marvin had stuck with weed, I thought, he'd have been fine. It was the pipe that did him in—that and his unchecked drive for self-destruction.

My drive was and is to keep writing. For the second time, I had to learn to keep hustling. After the publication of *Brother Ray*, I was sure that Stevie Wonder or Al Green would call to ask me to ghost their books. Those calls never came. *Divided Soul* received more attention than *Brother Ray*. Surely big-name stars would now seek me out. They didn't.

Marvin, though, had personally and persuasively introduced me to Christ consciousness. When he was in his right mind, I could feel it emanating from his soul. It was palpable. Real as rain. Sweet as sugar. Calming as sunset. Yet for all that calming—all that love-centric allure—there was an excitement to worshipping Jesus. I felt that same excitement when, a decade later, I began collaborating with an artist whose voice I loved with as much boundless passion as the voices of Marvin and Ray. Because she was the daughter of an illustrious preacher and the product of the golden age of gospel, I was convinced that our relationship would be deeply spiritual. Working with Ray was great; working with Marvin was even greater. But this would be the greatest of all.

Or would it?

THE
QUEEN

RAY CHARLES INTRODUCED ME to Aretha Franklin in his dressing room after one of his Los Angeles shows. That was 1977, when I was still working on Ray's book. I was thirty-four; Aretha, thirty-five. She was by then, of course, into her second decade as a great international star. I asked immediately if she had any interest in doing her own book, and, without thinking twice, she said no. She was curt and cold. That hardly mattered to me. I viewed Aretha like I did Ray and Marvin, as a deep and mysterious genius. And her style was like theirs: forged in the full-tilt gospel black church. As a young girl singing at her famous preacher father's services, she was celebrated as a prodigy. Her sound sent me reeling. The sheer thrill of her voice changed the chemistry inside my brain. Pain was in her voice. Joy was in her voice. God was in her voice. I couldn't hear that voice enough. I had to meet her. I had to tell her story. I was determined not to fail to put her voice on the page.

That determination was tested over the next seventeen years, when, despite my many furious supplications—phone calls, letters, postcards, faxes—she never once responded. Yet I remained hopeful because two books I had written brought me closer to her world. The first was Jerry Wexler's autobiography. Once a music journalist, Jerry had a soft spot for writers. He was the renowned producer who had brought Aretha Franklin to Atlantic Records in 1966 and convinced her to drop the pop approach she'd followed with middling success during six years on Columbia. Wexler pushed her to pursue the kind of gritty soul music he had made with Ray Charles and Wilson Pickett. No Wexler, no "Respect."

Jerry was an old-school New York intellectual. Nothing pleased him more than verbally destroying an adversary on matters of art or modern American fiction. He was self-absorbed and in need of constant adulation. He was a stone nonbeliever. He had no patience for my flirtation with Christianity, calling it foolish and misplaced, even though he had produced one of Bob Dylan's most openly Christian albums, *Slow Train Coming*.

"I liked the irony of Dylan coming to me, the Wandering Jew," said Wexler, "to get the Jesus feel. When he started to evangelize me, though, I set him straight. I said, 'Bob, you're dealing with a cranky sixty-two-year-old confirmed atheist. I'm hopeless. Let's just make an album.'"

Though in many ways Jerry mirrored Milton Ritz, unlike my dad, he had attained wealth and cultural fame. Ghosting his book, I became his son, his alter ego, and himself. He had endorsed a roman à clef I had written about a character that combined Aretha and Diana Ross. Ironically, the novel, *Glory*, published in 1979, was about a white Jewish writer trying to convince a black female superstar that he was her ideal biographer.

When I collaborated with Jerry on his 1993 memoir, *Rhythm and the Blues: A Life in American Music*, I thought that would bring me closer to the real Aretha. Jerry did, in fact, try to put me in touch—but to no avail.

Smokey Robinson, who had grown up around the corner from Aretha, also tried to help. While I was ghosting his autobiography, *Smokey: Inside My Life*, in 1989, we became friends. Smokey was as candid as he was cordial, a smooth and sinuous voice that I delighted in channeling. Smokey had recently put down a near-lethal cocaine addiction through his Christian faith. Our spiritual discussions were deep. He knew Marvin had paved the way, and he was more than ready to take me to the water. I wasn't ready.

"Why?" he asked.

"I have doubts," I said.

"No doubt, no faith. Blind faith isn't real. Faith that over-comes doubt is the strongest faith."

Smokey wanted the specifics of my doubts. I wasn't prepared to go into my theological permutations. My job was to write Smokey's book, not go off on tangents of my own.

"It takes as long as it takes," said Smokey. "But you'll get there."

"How do you know?"

"I feel it. I see the Lord doing a work inside you."

That statement gave me goose bumps. I couldn't explain why, but I knew he was right. Yet I still wasn't prepared to do anything about it. Too much to deal with. Just stay with the writing. Get Smokey to put in a good word with Aretha.

He did, but nothing happened until 1994, when I came to Detroit to research a novel I was plotting. Before leaving LA, I had sent Aretha a postcard, saying that I would be at the Atheneum Hotel and would love to talk to her. That was standard operating procedure. Every time I'd gone to Detroit before, I let Aretha know ahead of time. As if she cared. Except this time she did.

The phone rang.

"Mr. Ritz?"

"Yes."

"This is Miss Franklin. I'm interviewing collaborators for my autobiography, and I wanted to speak with you."

I gulped. This was no joke. It was *her*. My first thought was that I was too excited to get out a word. My stutter would do me in. And while I did stutter like crazy, I was not done in. Not yet.

"Thank you . . . Miss Franklin."

I thought of calling her Aretha, but the formality of her tone stopped me.

"I want to know how you'd go about working with me," she said.

"I'd be glad to come see you whenever it's convenient."

"I'm not doing in-person interviews. Just phone calls."

"So this is it?" I asked.

Her laugh let me breathe.

"Yes, Mr. Ritz, this is it. Explain your approach."

For the next forty-five minutes, I let loose with every last ounce of salesmanship at my command. With the phone at my ear, I paced the room, saying, "This collaboration will not only be a beautiful experience but one which you, Aretha . . ."

"Miss Franklin," she corrected me.

"Yes, you, Miss Franklin, will be in complete control and have final veto power over the manuscript. You will enjoy the experience. You will be intricately involved in helping me channel your voice. You will realize that the research I've already done on your music and life story over these past decades gives me a special qualification."

She already knew about that research. She knew that I had written Smokey Robinson's book, the same Smokey who had grown up around the corner from the Franklins and was best friends with Aretha's brother and longtime manager, Cecil. She knew that Cecil and I had become friends. She knew I had written the book for her most important producer, Jerry Wexler. She also knew that I had grown close to her sisters, Erma and Carolyn, both of whom I had interviewed over the years. Beyond that, I had already interviewed key figures such as John Hammond, the man who recorded a teenaged Aretha at Columbia Records, as well as Narada Michael Walden and Luther Vandross, two other critical Aretha producers from the 1980s and 1990s. Perhaps my greatest source of information was my good friend Ruth Bowen, who had served as Aretha's confidante and booking agent for thirty years.

"This is the book I've been working toward my entire life," I said.

"I understand, Mr. Ritz," Aretha said. "Thank you for your time. Good evening."

That was it. What followed was a week of agony. I tried calming down myself with the poetry of T. S. Eliot. I had long loved the cadences of his "Four Quartets." As with black gospel music, I realized that Eliot's art was rooted in Christ, but because of his poems' extravagant beauty—apart from their theology—I could embrace his aesthetic entirely. Over and over again I read his "Ash Wednesday," reciting out loud the lines that became my prayer: "Teach us to care and not to care / Teach us to sit still."

I believed the prayer but couldn't entirely submit to its wisdom. I cared passionately and, rather than sit still, I paced endlessly. When the word finally came—that Aretha had chosen me—it was one of the happiest moments of my life. Anointed by the Queen!

One of the first people I called with the good news was Billy Preston, the singer-songwriter-keyboardist who, like Aretha, had been mentored by the Reverend James Cleveland, a man I had profiled for *New West* magazine. James and Billy knew Aretha well. "Keep your hopes high and expectations low," said Billy.

"Why do you say that?" I asked.

"Because I know her, and girlfriend ain't giving it up. Ever."

I called Erma Franklin for encouragement. I had met Erma through her contemporary Etta James. Erma was a fine singer herself. Her original version of "Piece of My Heart," in 1967, was the template for the breakthrough single the following year by Big Brother and the Holding Company, featuring Janis Joplin. Younger sister Aretha, though, had overshadowed Erma's career. A woman of strong character, Erma went back to school, got her credentials, and became a social worker, dedicating her life to rehabilitating disadvantaged children.

"I love my sister dearly," she said, "and my prayers are with you. Nothing would make me happier than to see her purge all that pain she's been through. But honestly, I don't see her doing that. She's built a wall around herself that no one's been able to climb over."

Jerry Wexler echoed Erma.

"She'll see it as a public relations project," he said. "She'll stay away from the tough stuff."

Luther Vandross told me the same thing.

"If you get too personal," he opined, "she'll hand you your head on a platter."

Yet my inexhaustible enthusiasm could not be extinguished. What Billy and Jerry and Erma and Luther didn't understand was my determination. I was prepared to dig deep into my soul and pull out every last morsel of charm that God had gifted me. Others might call her the Ice Queen, but my warmth would melt the ice. I'd be so patient, so understanding, such a sympathetic listener that her protective wall would come tumbling down. Hadn't I worked with other difficult people? Ray Charles wasn't a walk in the park. Neither was Marvin Gaye. I had learned to ingratiate myself. And if I had to tiptoe around Aretha's tulips, I would do just that. I'd find her voice. I'd stimulate her candor. I'd make her proud. I'd make her happy. I'd serve the Queen with passionate integrity. I'd write the best book ever.

A month or so after my assignment was confirmed, I flew to Detroit. The night before I was scheduled to meet her at her Bloomfield Hills home, I drove by just to make sure that I knew the way. I didn't want to risk getting lost and being late. On the morning of our meeting, I arrived fifteen minutes early. Set upon a low-rising hill, the house was a white, sprawling, single-story structure built in an undistinguished semimodern style of the seventies. A limousine was parked in the driveway. Walking to the entryway, I spotted Aretha watching me from a side window. She opened the door before I had a chance to ring the doorbell.

She was wearing black pants, an extremely tight beige sweater, and a black, curly wig that fell to her shoulders. I arrived with no agenda. My first thought was to offer a prayer. The daughter of a preacher would surely welcome such a gesture. Besides, my heart was filled with gratitude that I wanted to express. I'd been praying for this gig for twenty years.

"Pray this time of day, Mr. Ritz?" Aretha asked skeptically. "Why don't we just sit and talk."

I saw that a formal prayer was too intimate of an act. So instead, I said simply, "I just wanted to thank God for giving us the chance to work together."

She offered a slight smile. I was disappointed. Aretha was not eager for a spiritual discussion.

Because I let that go, our initial meeting went well. My plan was to just let the conversation flow. Mainly we spoke of music. She was happy to describe her experience as a young singer who went on the road with her father and performed before his sermons. I loved listening to her description of the 1950s' golden age of gospel. She toured with many of the same groups I had heard as a teenager in Dallas: the Swan Silvertones, the Caravans, and the Staple Singers. She appreciated my passion for the musical culture that defined her style. We got along beautifully.

On the walls of her living room were large photographs of her charismatic father in his prime next to portraits of Aretha herself as a young ingénue, the tiara-crowned Queen of Soul.

"My childhood was beautiful," she said.

From speaking to her siblings, I knew it was painful and complex. Her parents divorced; her mother left the family and moved from Detroit to Buffalo, where she died when Aretha was ten; Aretha got pregnant at twelve and again at fourteen; before her fifteenth birthday, she had given birth to two sons. These were subjects I knew had to be addressed, but I also knew there was no hurry. I proceeded slowly.

Aretha put a plan in place: she would call me when she wanted to fly me to Detroit for the interviews. At times, she said, I could come to her recording sessions or meet her on the road. However, her fear of planes severely restricted her travel, and her performance schedule was light. She liked to stay home, and I liked visiting there.

Sometimes the trips could be challenging. Once, Aretha asked me to arrive on Monday. She called on Tuesday to say that her beauty appointment meant postponing our interview to Wednesday. When I didn't hear from her on Wednesday, I left her a voice mail but didn't hear back until Thursday, when she said it was too close to the weekend to start working. Would I mind returning to Detroit in a couple of weeks? Gritting my teeth, I said that I didn't mind at all.

Aretha struggled with organization. After the death of her brother, Cecil, from a heart attack in 1989, there was no manager she trusted. "I manage myself," she was quick to say. On the road, she paid her singers and musicians in cash. No receipts, no tax forms. She never went onstage without carrying her purse and placing it close to her. She went over her own contracts with a fine-tooth comb and was continually firing one lawyer and hiring another. Aretha could be generous, but doing her own bookkeeping was disastrous. She was negligent in her payments. Lawsuits from her creditors resulted in a page-one exposé in the *Detroit News*.

Sometimes her disorderliness turned comical. For example, she invited me to a Fourth of July picnic at her home, where a team of caterers and servers arrived with large platters of food. The party was slated to start at one o'clock. At two, I was the only guest. It was then that Aretha glanced over at the pile of invitations still sitting on the desk in her study.

"Uh-oh," she said without any consternation. "I guess I forgot to put the invitations in the mail."

She phoned a few friends who lived down the street. Five of us sat down to a meal meant for fifty. After dinner, in a surprisingly upbeat mood, Aretha called me into the den to interview her about how her mother and grandmother had taught her to cook. For the rest of the week, feasting on the picnic leftovers, we continued to talk about food.

My favorite spot was the kitchen. That's where Aretha was most relaxed. She took pride in her cooking. She liked making me fried chicken and waffles, lasagna, and banana pudding. It was always comfort food. The kitchen was also where Aretha laughed most readily. She liked jokes and delivered punch lines with flair. While serving up her signature hot-water cornbread, she told funny back-in-the-day stories of growing up as the daughter of a man who, to her way of thinking, was overprotective. She and Erma snuck out of the house to see soul singer Little Willie John; she took sister Carolyn to see doo-wop groups like the Flamingos and the Penguins. The even more compelling stories, though, were about the artists her father hosted in the Franklin home: jazz singer Dinah Washington and bluesman B. B. King, jazz immortal Duke Ellington and pianist Oscar Peterson.

A cultural progressive, Reverend C. L. Franklin rejected the traditional notion that secular and sacred music were incompatible. He loved the blues, he loved jazz, and he ultimately encouraged his daughter to sing both. He saw the possibility of her becoming an international star and did everything in his power to make that happen.

She talked about how the two of them watched Al Jolson's *The Jazz Singer*, the film in which the Jewish cantor, a singer of sacred songs, renounces his son for singing secular music.

"My father loved being called Rabbi," said Aretha. "And we both loved Al Jolson."

"Most preachers would discourage their children to sing secular," I said. "Many ministers of your father's generation viewed rhythm and blues as the devil's music."

"My father was different. He was enlightened. He was without that old-fashioned prejudice. He knew it was all God's music. And besides, he loved show business and show business people. After all, he was a star himself."

I saw this as an opening to discuss other parts of her childhood, such as her parents' divorce.

"It was amiable. Mother moved to Buffalo, where I often visited."

I told Aretha that her siblings had spoken to me about their dad's violent temper and his reputation as a ladies' man. "Lies!" she snapped. "Nothing but lies. You've asked enough questions today. This session is over."

And so it went.

A few weeks later, when the issue of her sons arose, I asked about the challenges of being a teenage mother.

"It wasn't a challenge at all," she said. "Big Mama, Daddy's mother, rose to the occasion and helped out."

"Was your father upset about your pregnancies?" I asked.

There was a great pause. I imagined the wheels spinning inside. This was nothing she wanted to discuss.

"My father was not upset" was all she said.

I doubted that statement, but realizing that my job was to keep the vibe between us cool, I could hardly challenge her. I could, however, ask about the fathers of her first two sons.

Aretha referred to them as Romeo and Casanova, refusing to reveal their first names.

"Why?" I asked.

"Why not?" she answered. "Like the song says, 'Ain't Nobody's Business.'"

I asked, did she consider marrying either man?

"Those weren't my thoughts," she shot back. "Now, let's move on."

When we finally approached her fabled marriage to Ted White—"a polished pimp," in the words of Aretha's contemporary, singer Bettye LaVette—she called the relationship insignificant. When I mentioned that her sisters and brother had spoken often of the physical abuse Aretha suffered at White's hands, she shut down the conversation. The same thing happened when I gently tried to approach the drinking and mental health challenges she faced in the sixties and seventies. "I have no interest in dwelling on negatives," she said, "when the positives are far more plentiful."

The interview phase of our collaboration lasted nearly a year. Aside from being chastised for bringing up sensitive subjects, I was able to avoid Aretha's wrath. Whenever the subject of music arose, the tone lightened. She loved comparing notes with me about jazz, blues, soul, and gospel artists. She was generous in her praise of other artists with the exception of certain female singers—Patti LaBelle, Gladys

Knight, and especially Natalie Cole—with whom she felt competitive. I made it a point not to mention them.

Our relationship soured when I began to actually write the book. She didn't like my style and, more importantly, didn't think I had captured her voice. Her complaint was that I was taking far too many liberties. She felt so emphatically about my misinterpreting her that she had her attorney call me.

"Miss Franklin has instructed me to inform you to write the book exactly as she is speaking to you," he said.

"But speaking isn't writing," I explained. "We don't speak prose."

"She wants you to quote her literally," he reiterated. "I cannot be any clearer."

"So I should just present her with the raw transcriptions?"

"I'm not a writer, Mr. Ritz. I'm an attorney. I'm merely telling you that this is Miss Franklin's book, and Miss Franklin wants to be quoted verbatim."

I did just that. I sent Aretha a section in which she discussed moving at age eighteen to New York, where she was booked into Greenwich Village jazz clubs. A week passed before I heard from her attorney again.

"Miss Franklin is not in the least pleased," he said. "She feels that you are ridiculing her."

"In what way?"

"The writing makes her sound discursive and incoherent."

"That's because they're verbatim transcripts."

"She feels that you continue to reconfigure her language in a way that does not properly represent her."

"Let me give it another try."

"Please do. But be warned: her patience is waning."

Because this was a gig I didn't want to lose, I was dead set on solving the dilemma. The only way to do that, though, was through a one-on-one sit-down with Aretha. When she agreed, I was relieved.

"Meet me in New York," she said. "I'm performing at the Grammys."

THE
CORONATION

THE WEEK STARTED OFF with dinner at Le Cirque, where, after the arrival of an extravagant assortment of haute cuisine entrees, Aretha pulled out a bottle of Lawry's seasoning salt from her purse. She sprinkled it on every dish. At evening's end, she retrieved a thousand dollars in cash from deep inside her cleavage, set the bills on the table, and took her leave.

The next night, at a charity event, Aretha sang Puccini's "Nessun Dorma" from *Turandot*. She'd been practicing the aria in Detroit with a vocal coach for months. The great Italian operatic tenor Luciano Pavarotti was present and praised her interpretation, inviting her to Italy. Together they would perform at La Scala, Milan's famed opera house. When she explained that she didn't fly, Pavarotti said he'd send a private plane "with a pilot that makes flying more soothing than taking a bubble bath." Aretha graciously accepted the offer but never made the trip.

The Grammys were three days later. Before that, she and I met for lunch. I was going to bring up the subject of her dissatisfaction with my work—except for the fact that she no longer seemed dissatisfied. She praised my descriptions of her father's fiery sermons and said that he was coming alive as a compelling character. She promised that when we got to Detroit, we'd do more interviewing about her early days at Atlantic Records. Miraculously, I was back in the Queen's favor.

On February 25, the fortieth annual Grammy Awards ceremony was held at Radio City Music Hall. Aretha sang "Respect" some thirty minutes before Pavarotti would be singing "Nessun Dorma." Then all hell broke loose.

Less than an hour before Pavarotti was to perform, he lost his voice. Producer Ken Ehrlich asked Aretha to take his place. Could she? Would she? She would, she told Ehrlich, if the orchestra was using the same arrangement to which she had the sung the aria at the charity event. Unfortunately, it was a different arrangement set in a different key. Was there a tape of the arrangement that she could hear? There was. She listened to it and then asked, "How much time do I have before you want me out there singing it?"

"Twenty minutes," Ehrlich answered.

Twenty minutes later, Sting reintroduced Aretha to the worldwide audience and explained the circumstance of her surprise substitution. In a red brocade dress with a mink collar and mink cuffs, she commanded the stage and, in spite of the unfamiliar orchestration, infused "Nessun Dorma" with the grit and glory of gospel soul. She had turned this last-minute substitution into a singular triumph.

"This was her greatest moment," Atlantic Records president Ahmet Ertegun told me. "This was her true coronation."

The next morning, Aretha was in an ebullient mood when she called to say it might be better not to meet her in Detroit because she was planning to come to California. I was shocked. Her bus trips had been restricted to the East Coast. Aretha had said that she was apprehensive about driving over the Rockies, and that the southern route was too long. But her Grammy performance had emboldened her, and, besides, the offers to sing in Los Angeles were too lucrative to pass up.

Three weeks later, she passed up those offers. She said the trip would be too grueling, and when I suggested that I come to Detroit, she demurred.

"I need to read more of the pages you've written," she said.

This time Aretha did not have her lawyer respond. She responded herself. She called me with many complaints. The language wasn't florid enough. The vocabulary was too limited. She liked longer paragraphs, and she did not like dashes. Commas were fine. Colons and semicolons were unnecessary. Certain words required italicization. There were not enough parenthetical phrases. Most important, though, was the voice. She indicated three or four specific passages where she did not recognize the voice as her own.

I didn't argue. In fact, I said I'd make the changes she requested and do my best to adjust the voice. I wanted to satisfy Aretha but was also concerned about those sensitive subjects—her dad's promiscuity, her many stormy relationships with men, her bouts with depression—that needed to be addressed. I did address those issues in a long letter to Aretha. I tried to write measuredly and gently. Certain facts, certain emotions, certain critical events were unavoidable and crucial elements of her story. I never heard back from Aretha personally. Once again she employed her attorney to speak for her.

"Miss Franklin would like you to complete the manuscript," he said, "following all her instructions to the letter."

What instructions? I was baffled but still determined to complete the job. I spent a month reworking the book in a tone that, at least to my ear, reflected Aretha's voice. I turned in the book. Weeks passed. Then months. And then finally word came down: Aretha had hired two private secretaries to work at her house while she read over my manuscript to them, making changes along the way. I was excluded from the editing process.

When *From These Roots* came out in 1999, I expected her to delete my name on the cover. She did not. I was credited as her collaborator. Reading her version of the book for the first time, I wished she had deleted my name. Although she retained many of the passages I had written—mostly those describing music—she had completely ignored those issues I had asked her to address. Her childhood read like a fairy tale. Her dedication was to her parents, who, she wrote, "came together in love and marital bliss and out of that union came I, Aretha." Her father was portrayed as a saint. Her struggles with men, drink, and mental health were barely mentioned. She gave them little or no significance. Having lived a breathtakingly dramatic life, she chose to eliminate the drama in her book. There was no self-reflection or revelation. In the same dedication, she praised herself: "If I have reached the goal of being a good mother, have been a guiding light and have inspired my sons to be proud, creative, independent, and productive citizens, then I have reached a priceless pinnacle in parenting."

Critics noted the book's superficiality, and, for the most part, buyers ignored it. When she appeared on *Oprah* to plug it, she squandered the opportunity by chastising Oprah Winfrey, as she had chastised me, for asking questions that were too personal. In the marketplace, the book sank like a stone.

I was crestfallen. I had contributed to a book that, in my mind, lacked depth and introspection. Yes, it was written in Aretha's voice, but a voice I found protective and, to some degree, false. At the same time, I consoled myself with the irrefutable truth about ghostwriting: there's only so much the ghost can do. It was Aretha's book, not mine, and she had every right to present herself to the world any way she saw fit.

Aretha never asked my reaction to her editing, and I never offered it. Our relationship remained cordial. Subsequently, when she released new albums, she called me to write press releases and short bios. I was glad that she seemed to have forgotten her displeasure with my writing. Essentially, she was now asking me to create ad copy for her. Since ad copy was right up my alley, I obliged. I liked staying in touch with the Queen. I suppressed my negative feelings about the book. A few months after its release, *From These Roots* was already forgotten. So why dwell on disappointment? Aretha liked her book. She was glad I had, at least in part, led her through the process. Her book was an accurate mirror of how she viewed herself. I decided to let bygones be bygones. And yet something gnawed at my soul. Aretha's story—at least the story I took to be true—remained untold.

TWELVE YEARS PASSED, and still *From These Roots* haunted me. It wasn't the bad reviews or disappointing sales. I had experienced that before. It was that, in my opinion, Aretha's character had not come alive. Even many of the basic facts of her life had been conveyed inaccurately. Making me even crazier was my conviction that I knew the story and needed to tell it. I had years of private time with Aretha plus years of researching her story before meeting her. I could tell the story not just from my perspective but also from the perspectives of those closest to Aretha.

Yet I knew the book, no matter how sensitive and discreet, would hurt her. I remembered an incident when her sister Carolyn was interviewed on national television, saying that after their father's death in 1984, the family was worried about Aretha, given how close she was to her dad. Aretha was infuriated and didn't speak to Carolyn for months. She took the comment as an attack on her mental stability. It didn't take much to enrage Aretha. The slightest criticism would trigger her.

My methodology—my entire career, in fact—has hinged on endearing myself to the people with whom I work. I want to please, not antagonize them. That doesn't mean I haven't challenged them. In the cases of Ray Charles, Marvin Gaye, Smokey Robinson, B. B. King, Etta James, and Buddy Guy, I felt free to push back when their stories seemed suspect or self-serving. Because I had gained their trust, they accepted those challenges and saw how an open exchange helps unearth the truth. Not so with Aretha. Challenges were regarded as insults. I knew that the only comprehensive book about her life would be one over which she had no control. Yet still I hesitated.

I saw myself as a ghost. I didn't want to be a biographer. I had learned that I'd rather work with artists on their books. I had written Marvin Gaye's biography only because his death had prevented the completion of his autobiography.

Yet this Aretha matter wouldn't go away. Years after our book came out, I went to Detroit to attend a gospel concert she was producing at New Bethel Baptist, the church that her dad had led. Afterward, she greeted me warmly and said she might be interested in doing another book with me. I was shocked. For a second, I thought she realized the mistake she had made and would be willing to be more forthcoming.

"I'd like to go back and review some of the earlier material," I said. "I'd like to do it more in depth."

"Oh, no," Aretha retorted. "*From These Roots* is perfect the way it is. I'm talking about everything that has happened since. *Rolling Stone* magazine named me the number one singer of all time. And then there are many, many awards I've received in the past few years."

"I think that a new edition would have to include more than just a listing of new honors."

"I don't agree," she said. "These awards didn't get the publicity they deserve."

When I introduced the idea of my writing an independent biography, she shot back, "As long as I can approve it before it's published."

"Then it wouldn't be independent."

"Why should it be independent?"

"So I can tell the story from my point of view."

"But it's not your story, it's mine."

"You're an important historical figure, Aretha. Others will come along to tell your story. That's the blessing and burden of being a public figure."

"More burden than blessing," she said.

Did I want to burden Aretha with revelations that would pain her? Or was I buying into her victimhood mind-set by presuming that the book would be a burden? My motive had nothing to do with injuring her and everything to do with honoring the complexity of her story. I was convinced my qualifications were unique. Before I started writing, I met face-to-face with three of her closet relatives: first cousin Brenda Corbett, who sang background for Aretha for three decades and grew up with her in the C. L. Franklin household; sister-in-law Earline Franklin, widow of Aretha's brother, Cecil; and niece Sabrina Owens, Erma's daughter. Each woman encouraged and helped me. "We trust you to write the *righteous* version," said Brenda.

I liked the word *version* because that's what it would be. That's what all biographies are. Autobiographies as well. I've come to believe that there is no such thing as a definitive version. Though the second book I eventually wrote on Aretha, the independent biography I called *Respect: The Life of Aretha Franklin*, was labeled definitive by some critics, I didn't buy that. My point of view, although well informed, was hardly objective. I brought my bias to the book. I allowed other witnesses to speak about her at length. But I was the one who chose those witnesses, and I was the one who determined which portions of their observations to include.

The book, published in 2014, was received enthusiastically. Most everyone saw that I did indeed love Aretha's artistry and tried my best to honor the nuances of her character. I mentioned her four children without telling their stories. It was their business to choose to do that, not mine. I discredited pernicious gossip that had been whispered for years. Everywhere I could, I gave voice to the people who were part of her life. It was, in fact, a biography, but one written by a veteran ghostwriter. I was far more interested in channeling voices other than my own, so much so that after reading the first draft, my editor at Little, Brown, John Parsley, urged me to insert more of my own voice.

I was proud of the book and not at all surprised that Aretha was furious. On several occasions, she made a point to bad-mouth me in public. She even threatened to hire a criminal lawyer. I was asked to respond to her angry interviews. All I said was, "I think the book is good. I think it's respectful. I think the portrait of her art and personality is accurate."

No lawsuit was filed, but, sadly, Aretha and I never spoke again.

When she passed on August 16, 2018, the nation mourned her as our most sacred singer. I went to Detroit to witness the final chapter. The spirit of celebration and civic pride was everywhere. She was greatly loved. She had managed to marry the three great strains of her heritage—gospel, blues, and jazz—into a sound both emotionally raw and technically refined. No one has ever been able to combine the glory of the gospel, the angst of the blues, and the sophistication of jazz with such impassioned sincerity.

Listening to Aretha, we feel visceral pleasure. We feel visceral pain. We feel a woman expressing pent-up emotions we ourselves are incapable of releasing. We feel ruthless honesty in a voice exposing the ragged condition of the unguarded heart; a voice whose sacred source makes an inaudible God audible; a holy voice combining a maze of contradictory elements into sensuous harmony; a voice forcing us to surrender to its frightening beauty; a voice that will continue to bring her impassioned fans deep and abiding solace.

"YOU DON'T KNOW 'BOUT THE BLUES, YOU LIVE 'EM"

ALIFETIME BEFORE I MET ARETHA, I understood how art provides solace. As a thirteen-year-old, I had discovered, in fact, that writing gave me solace. When I wrote articles for my junior high school newspaper, I found a voice I could like. I also found a way to assuage the immediate pain caused by my speech impediment. I laughed at myself, allowing others to do the same. Now I see it as a form of suppressing the shame. Then I saw it as emotional survival.

Yet for all my self-deprecating humor, a strong silent sense of verbal inadequacy remained. When I wrote, though, the inadequacy vanished. I didn't live with the fear that words would get stuck in my throat. I wrote effortlessly. I felt free. I never experienced writer's block—not then, not ever. And never once did any of my teachers say that my voice on the page did not accurately reflect my real voice. No one expected me—no one ever expects a stutterer—to stutter on the page. Thus, I found myself writing in a make-believe voice, an idealized voice, that, looking back, created a kind of fiction of myself as a fluent speaker.

I presumed that all the literary voices I was learning to love as a young student—Ernest Hemingway and James Baldwin, Jack Kerouac and Allen Ginsberg—were also artificial inventions.

"Writing is art," my father explained, "and while art reflects reality, that reflection is poetic. It can be concrete or abstract, it can be beautiful or terrifying, but it's always artifice. Its artfulness depends upon a ruse."

I saw that ruse as reinvention—an act that thrilled me. Yet far more thrilling than the literary voices I was hearing in my head were the musical voices I heard on the radio, on records, and in the clubs I frequented.

Their voices were distinct, and they were conversational. They were urgent, they were funny, they were sad, they were vulgar, they were captivating, they were joyful. They were filled with longing. They were deeply sexual. I never doubted the truth of their emotional expression. To my ears, these were authentic voices devoid of pretense. They seemed un-checked, uncensored, and defiantly ungrammatical.

So now I had fallen in love with two forms of voices, two different projections and reflections of speech: the literary and the musical. And while I heard undeniable authentic-ity in the voices of writers and singers, what about my own voice? How would I find it?

My first reaction was to reject the voice that had formed me: my father's. In my teens, I turned against him, partly be-cause of his inappropriately using me as his confidant. He had no notion of the importance of child-parent boundaries. He thought that telling me about his secret lover strength-ened our bond. Instead, it nearly destroyed it. Maybe he didn't realize how this information would burden me. Or maybe his narcissism prevented him from caring.

I was tired of his pontifications on literature, art, and politics. His need to be right, to wield his intellect like a sword, to tell the same tired stories of his radical past and friendships with famous writers—it all repelled me. By ques-tioning him more pointedly, I also discovered that he hadn't read all the books he claimed to have mastered. I saw him as a fraud.

I challenged my father. I called his bluff. I called him names. I was furious at discovering his feet of clay. All this happened at an especially stressful time. He had lost his job as a hat salesman and was scuffling.

Our move to Dallas in the midfifties also brought on a musical break between me and my father. Dallas was all about the rhythm and blues, a genre about which he had only cursory knowledge. I loved R & B. The blues, though at the root of the complex bebop I had come to revere in New York, was served up raw in Texas. My father never really understood raw rhythm and blues.

While still in high school, I went to see the Ike and Tina Turner Revue in a small club in Fort Worth. They slayed me. I loved the head-spinning sexuality of Tina and the Ikettes, the scantily clad singer/dancers with their glittering miniskirts, their long legs, their whirling ponytails. Ike's small band had the snap, crackle, and pop of Basie. Dallas offered up all sorts of R & B riches, electric guitar geniuses such as Freddie King, whose vicious licks felt like razor blades slicing my heart.

As editor of the *Thomas Jefferson Reveille*, the school paper, I convinced the faculty advisor to let me interview Jimmy Reed, the great bluesman who bridged the gap between backcountry and big-city blues. Even the white boys with their crew cuts had Reed's "Big Boss Man" and "Baby What You Want to Do" blasting from their Chevy Bel Airs.

In April 1958 I set out to meet Reed at his gig at LuAnn's, a cold and characterless dance hall that smelled of Lone Star beer, Fritos, and refried beans. That night, he rocked hard. His hypnotic, mantra-like groove, his slurry, sassy, nasty, nasal voice, his crying harmonica, his visceral pain, his hallelujah-tonight's-the-night jubilation—I loved it all, along with his astounding look: leopard-skin guitar at his chest, gleaming gold harp at his mouth, slicked-back hair, razor-thin mustache, sky-blue suit, fire-engine-red tie, white buck shoes. "Got me running, got me hiding," he sang. "Got me dizzy," he sang. Song after song, every note sounding the same yet different, tougher, louder, lewder and cruder. He had me crazy.

After his last song, I made my way to the bandstand, gathered up my courage, and faced the man himself.

"Excuse me, Mr. Reed, but could I interview you?"

"Come on," he said.

He motioned me to follow him and a curvaceous lady in a pink, skin-tight velvet gown. We all got into the back of a limo, which quickly pulled away. I had no idea where we going and didn't care. I was with Jimmy Reed.

I had my questions prepared. What was it like growing up in rural Mississippi? What was his relationship with other

legendary guitar players such as Elmore James? What was
the methodology of his songwriting? How did he process his
success among white teenagers? As I prepared to ask my first
query, he fished a flask from his suit pocket and drained it
dry before asking the driver for a beer chaser.

"What about me?" asked his woman. She was only a few
years older than me yet was stunningly self-assured. As she
crossed her legs and locked eyes with Jimmy, I felt her heat.

"Nothing for you," said Jimmy. "I saw you dancing out
there."

"Dancing with the promoter," she said. "Gotta be nice to
the promoter."

"Gotta be nice to no one but me," he shot back before
turning his attention to me. "Now, what is it you want to
know, youngblood?"

Before I could answer, the lady broke in with more sass,
saying, "I'll be nice to whoever I wanna. That's how you work
it. No reason for me not to work it that way too."

Rather than reply, Reed whipped out a razor and in one
quick motion cut the woman on her upper arm. She screamed
and went after him with her fingernails, long as knives, and
caught his chin. He smacked her back. She landed on the
floor. Blood gushed from her arm. Blood dripped down Jimmy's chin. Next thing I knew, we were pulling up to the emer-
gency room of a hospital. The driver was completely cool,

as though this were a common occurrence. He and I sat in the waiting room for hours. Finally, at three in the morning, Jimmy and his lady emerged. They wore bandages and were also holding hands.

Reed acknowledged my presence by saying, "Let's have breakfast."

At an all-night diner, we sat in a booth, the four of us facing a mountain of bacon and biscuits.

"Now, what is it you wanna know?" he asked.

I couldn't remember any of my prepared questions and instead simply confessed, "I guess I just wanna know about the blues."

Taking a big bite of pancake soaked in egg yolk, Jimmy Reed answered, "You don't know 'bout the blues, you live 'em."

MORE BLUES CAUGHT UP WITH ME in Austin, Texas, in the form of Lightnin' Hopkins, whom I heard in a small coffeehouse on Guadalupe Street, the main college drag. It was the early sixties, and I had enrolled at the University of Texas at Austin. Lightnin' later gained fame as an avatar of country blues, but, at the time, was playing for tips. He started off the first song not by singing but by narrating a story about a small orphan boy whose stutter wins the sympathy of Mr. Charlie, who hires the youngster to watch over his sawmill. The boy's only job is to warn Mr. Charlie if the mill catches fire. When it does catch fire, the boy runs to Mr. Charlie, but his stutter prevents him from saying the words.

"If you can't say it," Mr. Charlie advises, "then sing it." That's when the story turns to song as Lightnin', playing the part of the little boy, is suddenly rendered fluent by the melody's urgent flow, singing out, "Whoa, whoa, Mister Charlie, your rolling mill is burning down!"

I was flabbergasted. All truth seemed contained in this simple song. All I could do was let Lightnin' show me the way to his Houston home, where I interviewed him for two straight days. My aim was to write a profile for my college paper. But when I tried to capture Lightnin's speaking voice, I stumbled. If I quoted him verbatim, he'd sound coarse and uneducated. He was both of those things, of course, but he was more. There was poetry in his backwoods patois that I was incapable of rendering. Could I twist his words around? Was that allowed? Could I invent quotes? Was I a reporter or a portrait painter? In either case, what rules applied? I was lost. My tepid profile of Lightnin' was rejected.

My next interview was with John Lee Hooker, the great Mississippi bluesman who had migrated to Detroit and gained fame with hits like "Boogie Chillen," "Crawling King Snake," and "Boom Boom." John Lee was a severe stutterer.

Given the speech impediments of both interviewer and interviewee, you can imagine the extended length of our discussion. I don't know whether it was my stutter or my openhearted admiration for his music, but John Lee liked me. He unlocked his heart, and his stories poured out. When I asked him why his songs usually didn't rhyme, he said that natural speech doesn't necessarily rhyme, and all he knew was natural speech. Before we said good-bye, he leaned over and asked, "W-w-w-w-w-hen you wr-wr-wr-wr-write this up, h-h-h-h-how you gonna have me talking?" I thought I knew what he meant, but I asked him anyway.

"You mean," I said, "will I d-d-d-d-d-escribe you as a s-s-s-s-tutterer?"

"I wouldn't like that," he said. "I think it'd be b-b-b-b-b-b-better if you had me talking n-n-n-n-n-normal. Bad enough folks g-g-g-g-g-gotta hear me talkin' this w-w-w-w-w-way in real life. But in b-b-b-b-b-book life, you can clean me up and s-s-s-s-s-mooth me out. Will you d-d-d-d-d-do that for me?"

I reminded him that he'd recorded a song, "Stuttering Blues," in which he reveals his stutter. He reminded me that he used his stutter to get a woman. "I t-t-t-t-old her," he said, "I c-c-c-c-c-can't get my words out the w-w-w-way I wanna, but I can sure g-g-g-g-g-get my l-l-l-l-l-l-lovin' out in a hurry."

We both laughed, and I promised him that I'd turn him into a smooth talker. I did, but in doing so, my characterization was off. The portrait I painted was bland. In trying to protect the bluesman, I had failed to capture his voice.

I was surprisingly comfortable hanging out with Lightnin' and John Lee. For all the vast differences, their earthy attitudes reminded of my mother's Lower East Side family. I saw the two musicians' love for the blues was absolute, just as firm and feverish as Mahalia Jackson's love for God. I wondered if the two—the blues and the divine—were connected. Something told me they were, but that "something" was still small as a mustard seed.

GOD'S GOT THE BLUES

B. B. KING HAD STOPPED playing gospel music—his first love—so he could make money singing the blues.

I was a boy when I met John Lee and Lightnin', but a man when I met B.B. In the nineties, I traveled with him the world over when I ghosted his autobiography *Blues All Around Me*. No matter how long the arduous journey, no matter how many overeager fans sought his attention, B.B. embraced patience like a preacher embraces prayer.

Touring the United States, he loved riding the bus from gig to gig. Most of our discussions took place in his back bedroom, where he'd set up a couch. Every afternoon, he stopped our interviews to listen to the music he loved best. It was a religious ritual. He played bluesmen T-Bone Walker, Muddy Waters, Little Walter, and Lead Belly for hours on end.

Our most moving set of interviews ensued while driving through the Mississippi Delta, B.B.'s home turf. At the time, I was reading Tolstoy's *War and Peace* and was especially touched by the novelist's depictions of the changing landscape of agrarian Russian. He wrote of the peasants' love of the land.

When I mentioned this to B.B., he related immediately.

"I was a sharecropper chopping cotton in those very fields," said B.B., nodding toward the window. "I knew it was the system left over from slavery. I knew the system was cheating me and my people, but the work itself . . . well, I actually liked it. Liked being close to the land. Liked seeing that white world of freshly bloomed cotton sprouting out every summer. A new crop was like a new life. I could see God's hand in the creation of the natural world. That made me wanna sing about him. Thank him for my life. Thank him for the rain that brought out the blossoms. Thank him for giving me the get-up-and-go to find a guitar and start plucking.

"Next thing I know, people are liking what I'm playing. So I'm sitting there on a wooden crate on a dirt road in Indianola, Mississippi, singing these gospel songs to the God that got me through. Mind you, this is the thirties—the deep bottom of the Depression, when no one's got a nickel. But folks are liking the way my songs are sounding, so they stop and say, 'That's it, son. You keep on praising God.' They say it and move on. I'm thinking, *Maybe they'll give me a few pennies*, but they don't.

"Then comes the day when I'm in that same spot, and, out of nowhere, I start singing a song by Lonnie Johnson, my favorite blues guy, called 'Hard Times Ain't Gone Nowhere.' Not five minutes go by before a man I know as a church deacon stops to listen. Don't say a word, but, man, that smile on his face says everything. Next thing I know, he puts his hand in his pocket, fishes out some loose change, lays out the coins in front of me, and, though he don't know it, the deacon changes my life."

B.B. became a bluesman because, as he said, "Blues meant money. And money meant a better life."

"And what about praising God?" I asked. "It sounded like a burning desire."

"It was," said B.B. "Still is. But then I figured something out. I ain't saying I'm a great thinker, but I did see my way clear to one idea that rings true clear as a bell."

"What is it?"

"This notion that God's got the blues."

"How do you know that?"

"Look at the story of Jesus. I'll be damned if that ain't a blues story. And I'll be damned if Jesus wasn't a bluesman. Wandering around. No home. No money. Yet all that time talkin' 'bout love. But not everyone's loving on him. Some folks be hating on him. Try as he might, he ain't winning over the world. World's on his back. Sitting in that garden, he knows the world's about to do him in. That's the blues, son. The sure-enough blues."

"But didn't he lose the blues when he supposedly went up to heaven?"

"To me—and remember, I'm just a country boy—he wouldn't love us, and we wouldn't love him if he ever lost the blues. That's the part of God that's human. Fact is, you could say that Jesus came down to earth to get the blues. You could say that's why God understands us."

I loved B.B.'s explanation but heard it as spiritual poetry—spiritual storytelling—as opposed to spiritual truth. Either way, his words stuck.

B.B. INTRODUCED ME to Buddy Guy, who, an astounding guitar virtuoso and great innovator himself, idolized King. Eleven years B.B.'s junior, Buddy was also the product of the agrarian South. He too had picked cotton and braved his way from the backwoods to the big city, where he, like King before him, became a great and enduring bluesman.

Buddy costarred with B.B. at a show in Baton Rouge, Louisiana, not far from where Guy had been raised. During their performance, they traded licks on their guitars. It was a musical conversation marked by wit and mutual respect. After the show, they sat on B.B.'s bus and talked women, wine, and song. The stinging back-and-forth of their verbal riffs echoed their guitar riffs.

"If it was back in the days when we were still wilding out," said Buddy, "we wouldn't be talking about this. We'd be doing it."

"Well, God took care of that, didn't he?" said B.B.

"What you mean?" asked Buddy.

"God never left us. He saw us take a turn this way or that, but he went along with us. He knew we were always coming back. And when we were wondering where he was—when we started to doubt—"

"—he showed up like the Lone Ranger, showed up to save the day," Buddy finished the thought.

"Saved my day for sure," said B.B.

"When I meet folk who say they don't believe in God," Guy reflected, "I say that I sure would rather put my faith in God than put my faith in man. Man is fickle. God is steady. God is the backbone of these blues we be playing.

He gave us these blues notes, told us to twist 'em up and turn 'em and let the world rejoice."

"Rejoice is the word," B.B. affirmed. "Can't remember any of the exact words preached to me back in that little country church where I first met the Lord, but I do remember the joy. Jesus is about joy. That joy got in the music—"

"—even when they called it the blues."

"*Especially* when they called it the blues!" said B.B. "'Cause the bluesmen, when they're playing, they're having a ball. So the joy is there, and so is Jesus."

Listening to this conversation, I felt my heart melting. I wanted to say that I too felt the joy of Jesus. But I stayed silent. I still wasn't ready to declare.

YEARS LATER, when Buddy hired me to ghost his own book, *When I Left Home: My Story,* he talked a lot about B.B., whom he considered a mentor.

"B.B.'s God-fearing," he said. "Can't say that about too many bluesmen. Many of them don't fear God 'cause they think they *are* God."

"I've always been struck by that phrase 'God-fearing,'" I admitted. "Do you think it's good to be afraid of God?"

"That's just how the old folk talked. I'm not believing that they feared God like they feared the Klan. They loved God, and that love is a lot stronger than any fear. Let me give you a for-instance: when my mama took a stroke, I was still a teenager. I wanted to hightail it up to Chicago, but I didn't wanna leave my mama. My heart was torn in two. Go to the big city and learn from the big blues cats; stay on the farm and care for the good woman who gave me life. That good woman, who called herself God-fearing, wasn't afraid of nothing. Not even this stroke that took away her speech. Came a day when I said to my daddy that I wanted to leave and I didn't want to leave. I wanted to ask Mama what she thought, but Mama couldn't talk.

"'Talk to her all the same,' said Daddy. 'She'll hear you. She'll let you know.' So I did. Went into her room where she was sitting up in bed, and I got real close. Told her I was scared to go and scared not to go. Told her I knew I had Daddy's approval, but that wasn't enough. Needed hers. But she couldn't say. Couldn't speak. 'If I go,' I promised her, 'I'll make enough money to buy you a polka-dot Cadillac.' Thought that might bring a smile to her face. No smile, no answer. I was crushed. I was more confused than ever until I fell asleep that night and saw this dream play out inside my head. I was lost in the woods. Then I saw Lightnin' Slim, this guitarist I loved, sitting in a rocking chair. Then came the shock. Bolt of lightning shattered the guitar. Woods caught on fire. I ran, thinking Mama and Daddy's house would burn down. When I got there, they weren't burned up. Mama and Daddy were clapping for me. They were clapping 'cause in my hand I was holding a spanking brand-new guitar. 'Keep playing, Buddy,' said Mama. 'Keep on playing.'

"That's when I saw that God had Mama talk to me in that dream the way she couldn't talk to me in real life. He used Mama just the way Mama had used him."

"How had your mother used God?" I asked.

"Used him to get our family through a dirt-poor life to a life lifted up by love. Used him to speak to me even when she couldn't. Used him to help me get past my fear so I could get on with my life. Don't you think he's using you the same way?"

I wanted to say yes, but I could say only that I wasn't sure.

PLEASE
SEND
ME
SOMEONE
TO
LOVE

PERCY MAYFIELD WAS A POET of the blues. He wrote "Hit the Road Jack" for Ray Charles. He also wrote and recorded one of the great enduring anthems in blues-ballad history, "Please Send Me Someone to Love," a plea that God grant him the gift of a girlfriend.

I met Percy in 1979 while I was working with Ray. By then, he was not in good shape. During a head-on car collision, his face had gone through the windshield, leaving a long, indented gash that extended from his hairline to the bridge of his nose. Once a handsome man, he now gave the appearance of a war survivor. His language was a concoction of lofty eloquence and salty street slang.

"A blues survivor," he called himself. "'Cause this blues business is a war. The business got a long and brutal history of beating down anyone looking for his fair share."

Percy's bitterness, based on his conviction that the music industry had cheated him out of untold millions and left him destitute, was offset by his sense of himself as a prophet.

"Prophet with a little *p*," he said. "Not a biblical prophet. A back-alley prophet. Been in these alleys my whole life, and I can say that if you think things are bad in our neighborhoods now, wait forty years and they'll be calling these the good ol' days. The danger zone is everywhere, and it's only getting worse as time goes by."

Mayfield's "Danger Zone," also sung by Ray, was a strange and haunting song in which he explained that in a world rife with peril, he clung to love because, in his words, "the world is a part of me."

I heard Percy sing the song when he invited Roberta and me to a dingy little club in South Central Los Angeles where he performed for tips. The place was half empty. There was no band. He sang acapella. There wasn't even a stage. Yet his presentation was riveting. He made us all feel as though we *were* in the danger zone. During a break, he came to our table and explained the song.

"Poetry's paradox," he said. "That's why the blues is poetry. Says one thing—'I'm blue'—but makes you feel another thing: 'I'm happy.' Same goes for this world. I'm blue to be in it. It's cold and cruel and don't care nothing 'bout me. But I'm also happy to be in it 'cause it's got pretty flowers and starlit skies and mechanical miracles that make your head spin 'round and your heart beat fast. You can see how the world's progressing. But along with progress comes bad behavior. Greed's growing like weeds, violence erupting like a volcano. And all the time, God is weeping 'bout how man is treating man."

"So it's a sad God you see," I said.

"He can't be happy. The genocide. The wars. The cruelty. How we treat the land. How we treat the animals. Not to speak about how we treat each other. Yes, sir, God's weeping. I like to think he's weeping to my songs."

"Is that why you write—to move God?"

"That's one reason. Another is how songs make order out of disorder. They give form to chaos. You dig? God does the same. That's his will. He wants us to make sense of nonsense. Nailing Jesus to the tree was nonsense. What did he do to deserve torture? Brother didn't do nothing. But deep down, Jesus knew what God knew. The nonsense made sense 'cause it showed us what love's all about. Sacrifice your child? I'd call that a mighty love. Mankind's prayer—

for salvation, for a way to get beyond the darkness of the grave, to conquer death—that prayer was answered forever and ever."

"So you're a big believer in prayers."

"I'm a big believer in songs. Just the way prophets wrote psalms, songs are my prayers. Don't matter if my congregation fills a football stadium or it's a few lonely souls in the barroom. They know I'm praying, and they pray along with me. Isn't that what you and Baby Sister are doing here tonight?"

Roberta's nickname, Baby Sister, came out of Percy's fondness for my wife. He'd had a lifetime of go-arounds with women and was adamant about giving me romantic advice.

"You better keep this one," he said, nodding at my wife. "You'd be a fool not to. She got everything you need—and then some. Don't you see? He sent you someone to love, and her name is Roberta."

I MET ROBERTA in Buffalo in 1967, when she was nineteen and I was twenty-three. I had gone to graduate school at the State University of New York because my father's friend, critic Leslie Fiedler, was on the faculty of the English Department and got me a teaching fellowship. My dear friend Lewis MacAdams, whom I knew from Dallas when we were both editors of our high school newspapers, turned up as well. Lewis was a poet and would go to on become a legendary environmentalist. He was a follower of the poet Charles Olson, whose acolytes had set up camp at SUNY Buffalo. I was a follower of Fiedler's Freudian/Jungian view of literature.

One Saturday night, Lewis insisted I abandon my obsessive study schedule and accompany him to an English Department party. There was Roberta, in an army-green denim shirt and black leggings, dancing to the Temptations' "Ain't Too Proud to Beg." I couldn't keep my eyes off her as she moved with easy grace. Lewis, far better at approaching women than I was, spoke with Roberta before calling me over to meet her. She had long, lustrous red hair that fell below her shoulders. Bangs covered her forehead, lending her a mysterious air. Her face was sprinkled with sweet freckles. Laryngitis had rendered her voice barely audible. I found that—just as I found everything about her—wonderfully sexy. Our banter was easy, as if we'd known each other forever. It turned out we had friends in common. She'd heard I had a good sense of humor. Humor was our first and forever bond. She'd grown up in the Forest Hills section of Queens, New York. Her background was like mine: working-class Jewish. Her mind was supple and her wit quick. We liked the same music (R & B and jazz), the same movies (Jean-Luc Godard and François Truffaut), the same authors (Jane Austen and Edith Wharton). She was clearly in the hippie camp. I liked dope and free love but had some reservations about the emerging Age of Aquarius.

"Well, maybe we should get away from this party," I suggested, adding boldly, "I can make you tea for your sore throat."

We went to my apartment on the top floor of a ramshackle building in a dicey section of midcity Buffalo. I did prepare her tea. I put on Billie Holiday's *Lady in Satin*, the most romantic suite of songs in my record collection. We found love that night. In the morning, when I walked her to the bus stop for her trip back to her dorm, she turned and said to me, "Take good care of the kids."

Somehow we both knew.

For the first time in my life, I was head over heels in love with someone who satisfied me on every level. Our intellectual rapport was as powerful as our physical rapport—and that's saying a lot. My history in this area was limited. I had enjoyed sexual liaisons with several boys in high school and college, yet those were more a matter of lust than romance. Before Roberta, I had two serious girlfriends, but neither relationship lasted long. Roberta and I had a soul connection that I had never felt before.

The summer after we met, Roberta, eager to experience the Summer of Love, went to San Francisco, where she lived in Haight-Ashbury and made candles. We spoke nearly every day. On July 4 Leslie Fiedler had his annual backyard party, where Allen Ginsberg spoke to me of his passion for jazz pianist Art Tatum. It was an exciting evening, but without Roberta, I felt desolate.

We were reunited in the fall, only to be separated again when I took off for Italy. I had won a scholarship to study at the University of Rome. After years of Italian classes, I was dying to get over there.

I found a cheap room in a pensione in the center of the city. I was so enchanted by Rome that I hardly noticed that no matter what time I returned to my room, the sheets were changed and my bed freshly made. Then one morning, after realizing I'd forgotten my notebook, I went back to fetch it. The owner of the pensione stopped me from going to my room and advised me to wait in the kitchen. Why? Curious, I went to my room anyway to find a couple making a hurried exit. The pensione was really an *albergo a ore*: a room rented by the hour for amorous purposes. My latent puritanism erupted. I moved out and found lodgings with an elderly woman, a professor emeritus of Greek tragedy.

In Rome, I was as exhilarated as I was despondent. I wandered the ancient ruins, shopped the modern department stores, hung out on the Spanish Steps to visit the home of the nineteenth-century English poet John Keats, where, at twenty-five, he took his final breath. I got hooked on espresso, discovered small jazz clubs in quiet corners of the city, and attended a concert where a pop singer named Mina, a long-legged chanteuse wearing a micro-miniskirt, unnerved me to where I became a lifelong devotee. Today I own every single and album the singer has ever recorded. I also saw seventeen-year-old Stevie Wonder, the miraculous man-child who turned a dance hall into a revival tent. I was crazed by his frenetic energy.

Yet without Roberta, Rome remained a lonely place. We corresponded feverishly, and I finally convinced her to leave school and come live with me. She arrived in a trench coat, her auburn hair spilling down her back, her eyes lit with love. By then, I had moved from the old professor's home into a small apartment on Via Baccina, a few feet from the magnificent Arco dei Pantani in the ancient center of the city. A few weeks later, I proposed to Roberta in the Michelangelo-designed Piazza del Campidoglio under the statue of Roman ruler Marcus Aurelius.

"Can I get back to you tomorrow?" she asked with a smile.

I didn't want a joke. I wanted an answer. The next day, she said yes.

Our relationship was never tepid. Roberta was volatile;

I was compulsive. Roberta slowly and painstakingly walked through museums, savoring each artifact; I treated museums as cardiovascular opportunities. I ran through them. In many ways, Roberta lived blissfully outside of time; I was madly punctual. Whatever the differences, she was my baby, and I couldn't see living life without her. She wrote beautiful poems. She loved Gladys Knight, Vivaldi, and Erik Satie. She taught me to appreciate Henri Rousseau's painting *The Sleeping Gypsy*.

Our idea was to return to Buffalo at the end of the semester so that she could complete her undergraduate work in English, and I could prepare for oral exams for my master's degree in English literature. We saw our wedding as a low-key ceremony at City Hall and nothing more. My mother, thinking I was acting impetuously, opposed the marriage. For the first and only time, she wrote me long letters warning me that I was making a wrong move. My dad said nothing. Mom's attitude did not dissuade me. She neither knew Roberta nor understood the depths of my feelings for her. I felt it imperative that I stand up for myself—and for Roberta—and let my mother know that, whether she liked it not, the marriage was on.

My mother seemed to accept my decision—so much so that we learned through a friend that she was planning a huge wedding party for us on Long Island; just the sort of gaudy affair we wanted to avoid. The invitations had already gone out—all without our knowledge. Roberta was incensed. Her attitude was plain: she wouldn't attend the party. I stood with Roberta. I insisted that my mother send out cancellation letters to all the invitees.

My parents met Roberta only a few days before our wedding in the office of a rabbi in a synagogue of New York's Upper West Side. My mother was cold as ice; my father was civil. The ceremony itself, attended only by Roberta's parents, my parents, and my grandmother Lena, was brief and painful. The rabbi, who did not know us, read a poem purporting to be a reflection of our love. It was not. My mother would not look Roberta in the eye. Afterward, the wedding party lunched at the Mayflower Hotel. I quickly developed close relationships with Roberta's mom and dad. Eventually my father warmed up to Roberta, but my mother remained distant and never forgave her for cancelling the wedding party.

Daunting domestic challenges loomed ahead.

THE
TERROR
OF
DEATH

E TTA JAMES LIKED TO TALK about love. Having suffered through a long series of ruinous relationships, she
thought herself an authority on the topic of romance. When I
introduced her to Roberta, they became instant friends. The
next day, Etta called me and, echoing Percy Mayfield, said,
"She's a keeper. I can see you love that girl."

I met Etta James through Jerry Wexler, who produced
two of her albums. Like Aretha, she had been a child
prodigy—a product of the full-gospel Baptist church, where
she became a star. Also like Aretha, she made an early switch
to rhythm and blues, and became an even bigger star. Her

1968 hit "Tell Mama" remains one of the great jewels of the golden age of soul.

When I met her in the eighties, Etta had yet to undergo the gastric bypass surgery that reduced her size dramatically. She was still a larger-than-life blues shouter who spoke as forcefully as she sang. She was also outrageously funny and candid. Her story was riveting: her mother, Dorothy, was a teenage prostitute who had abandoned her; Etta was convinced that her father was pool shark Minnesota Fats, one of Dorothy's clients. Later, she reunited with her mother, only to learn that Dorothy, an aficionado of the sophisticated jazz singing of Sarah Vaughan and Ella Fitzgerald, looked down on Etta for singing raucous R & B. Etta had been through lots of men and decades of torturous drug addiction.

Etta was a mess, but a beautiful mess of conflicting emotions: the drive to raise her two sons right; the impulse to buck all authority; the need to shock her audience; her determination to mock the stuffed shirts and laugh at life; her affinity for bluesy, rootsy rock; her commitment to sing the jazz she knew would please Dorothy (which she finally did in a series of records, starting with 1994's *Mystery Lady: Songs of Billie Holiday*).

"I'm schizophrenic to the bone," Etta told me when we first started our interviews for *Rage to Survive*, her autobiography, "so if I bark at your questions or tell you to get lost, don't pay me no mind. I'll be different tomorrow."

On one such tomorrow, we were in Boston, sitting in her hotel suite with a view of a nineteenth-century church.

"Look at all those spires," she said. "Takes me back to when I was a little girl singing at the St. Paul Baptist Church in LA. Choir was called the Echoes of Eden. How 'bout that for a name? Loved that choir and loved the choirmaster, Professor James Earle Hines. Professor had him a wife, but, believe me, he was gay as a goose. All the cats in the choir were gay as geese. Men with beautiful voices. So beautiful I called them angels. Called Professor the Big Angel. Called him that 'cause he led me to the Lord."

"How so?"

"Simple," said Etta. "He said God was in the song. 'You get in the song, Etta,' he said, 'and you'll be with God.' So when I got in the song, and all this warm feeling came over me, all this excitement, all this spirit, I knew to call it God. I knew the Holy Ghost had come down and landed on me. Later on, when I was shooting dope instead of singing, it made sense that the Holy Ghost was staying away. I was pushing that spirit away. But soon as I clean up, here comes the Holy Ghost to say 'Hey, Etta, where you been? Good to have you back, girl.'"

Etta, who loved to turn the tables during these interviews, asked me, "What about you and the Holy Ghost? He ever come for a visit?"

"I don't think so."

"I know so. Every time you start playing me some old Billie Holiday jam you think I should know about, I see you get all Ghosted up. He's all up in you. You just don't know what to call him."

"Is that important?"

"Sure, names are important. I wouldn't be happy if you called me Ella instead of Etta. Besides, who's ever come up with a better name than the Holy Ghost? That's some pretty poetry, ain't it?"

I didn't argue. I also didn't resist when Etta would entreat me to pray with her. She did the praying. I did the listening. I loved her prayers because they were no different from her ordinary speech. She spoke to God like he was right there in the room.

"Lord," she'd say, taking my hand and closing her eyes, "you know what I'm going through. You seen me popping those feel-good pills that I shouldn't be popping. You hear me making all these excuses that I'm taking 'em for medical reasons. You know that's bull. You know I'm playing with fire. You don't gotta tell me that. You see my boys getting in some trouble too. But they're good boys and don't mean no harm. They'll be all right, Lord, I can tell you that. They've had to put up with me, and that ain't easy, but it's beautiful to have my sons playing music. Same gift you gave me you gave them. Thank you, Jesus. Thank you for all these gifts. If I've abused them or neglected them or taken them for granted, I know you'll forgive me even though I don't deserve no forgiveness. But the good preachers—the righteous ones—say it ain't about deserving. You give gifts 'cause that's just who you are. You give love 'cause that's all you can do. You forgive my misbehavin' 'cause you can't do nothing but forgive. Don't understand why you're that way, but I'm glad you are. I know you are. If you weren't you, I'd be a crazy woman. I'm crazy enough as is, but I mean really, truly drown-in-a-sea-of-sorrow crazy. I don't need to tell you all this stuff, Lord, because you already know everything, but I'm saying it to make me feel better. So thanks for listening and letting me feel better. I'm going to stop pill-popping and pretending it's not dope, 'cause dope is dope, and dope is always trying to kill me while you're always keeping me alive with love."

Then Etta asked me if I wanted to pray. I did. I wanted to pray with Etta's unabashed sincerity; I wanted to pray with her utter lack of self-consciousness. I wanted to spill my guts and tell God about my desire to feel his love the way Etta felt his love. But instead, I demurred.

"You prayed for both of us" was all I could say.

"You also need to pray for your wife," she said. "You need to pray for a way to keep your marriage together. I can see the craziness in your eyes, and craziness in men's eyes ain't all that good for a marriage."

ETTA'S ASTUTE OBSERVATION took me back to the sixties, when, after we married, Roberta and I returned to Buffalo as planned. She completed her studies, and I passed the oral exams for my master's degree. It was 1968, the year of the assassinations of Dr. Martin Luther King Jr. and Robert Kennedy. The Vietnam War was raging. The brutal world that Percy Mayfield had lamented in his song "Danger Zone" was staring me in the face. When I was offered a teaching post at the University of Parma, in Italy, the choice was easy. Both Roberta and I wanted out of Dodge.

Situated between Milan and Bologna, Parma was a universe away, far from the confusion of an America in torment. The area was famous for cheese, ham, and opera. Giuseppe Verdi was born in the area and Toscanini in the city itself. It felt like an ideally studious spot to start writing my PhD dissertation on William Wordsworth while Roberta could continue her own fine poetry. She also found work tutoring young Italian students in English.

Parma was elegant in the extreme. When I first saw the Piazza del Duomo with its achingly beautiful baptistery, I wanted to hug it. Over one of its portals, the blue-gowned Blessed Virgin held Jesus with one hand and a blooming flower in another. The interior dome was awash with opaque Byzantine frescoes telling ancient stories of spiritual searches.

The city of 150,000 had just enough urban buzz to excite me and enough provincial chill to calm me. I saw Mina, my Italian Dinah Washington, perform at the local concert hall. I learned to love opera and soccer.

Roberta and I lived down the street from the music conservatory in a fifteenth-century palace that had been chopped up into apartments. Our bedroom felt like a ballroom. I taught classes in Italian and American literature and was hired to give weekly lectures at the University of Cremona, still another enchanting city an hour away in our little Fiat 500. Weekends in Milan, holidays in Venice. Life was sweet. Until the fog hit.

In wintertime, Parma and Cremona are buried under a blanket of fog. Fog so thick that you can't see a foot ahead. Fog so impenetrable that it's impossible to drive or even walk without risking danger. Dark fog filled with a chilling humidity that threw me, unexpectedly, into a state of terror. Fog that made me feel like the sun had died and, along with it, all possibilities of joy. Fog that brought me back to that moment in my childhood when my father had explained the finality of death.

"The lights go off," he said.

I often wonder how my psychic life would have changed had he said, "The lights never go off. They only get brighter."

In Parma, I never broke down on the outside—I continued to teach—but inside I was a mess. I was among the walking wounded. Fear of mortality never left me. Looking for light, I haunted Milan's Galleria Vittorio Emanuele II, built in the nineteenth century as the original shopping mall—a majestic space brimming with chic boutiques—yet I still felt traumatized. All these excited shoppers would eventually die. The laughing children would die. The gawking tourists would die. The shop clerks would die. I would die. The fog would never lift.

Roberta was loving and understanding, but there was little she could do. I couldn't shake my morbidity. Maybe Mozart's *Còsi Fan Tutte* would help. How could I resist a comic opera with heavenly, lighthearted melodies and a happy ending? But as I sat there in Milan, in the midst of the splendor of La Scala, the fog failed to lift. I read Theodore Dreiser's notion in his novel *Sister Carrie* that "Fears and misgivings wax strong, but out in the sunlight there is, for a time, cessation even of the terror of death." Well, there was sunlight in Rome, so we went there for several weekends, but even in the Eternal City where our love had blossomed, fear clung to me like a fever.

Fear took a specific turn: that, with an ocean between us, I would never see my parents again. This was a strange and new fear. Dad and I had been fighting for years; Mom's antipathy for Roberta had infuriated me. Nonetheless, I felt like a little boy in need of his mommy and daddy. I needed to get home and be close to them. Then and only then would the specter of death start to fade.

Back in Parma, I sat in the Sanctuary of Santa Maria della Steccata, a Renaissance church. I imagined Mahalia Jackson singing at the altar, "God is real because I feel him in my soul." Except that I didn't feel him. I felt only gnawing anxiety.

I didn't write a word of my PhD dissertation. The idea of academia lost its luster. I remember the words of my friend the poet Irving Feldman, who had told me, "You're too enterprising to become a scholar. I see you out there in the world, not trapped in stilted university life."

A master's degree was enough. I couldn't bear the notion of spending a year analyzing the works of a dead poet. I needed something different, something daring.

Roberta and I took a Sunday stroll through Parma's Parco Ducale, a once manicured royal garden fallen into neglect. Among the weeds, though, butter-yellow wildflowers were plentiful. Roberta pointed them out as signs of hope. Her hopeful heart meant the world to me. I wanted to adopt her viewpoint, but I was still covered in fear. We sat on a bench that faced a pond where a black mama duck swam by, her ducklings by her side.

"I think we need to get out of here," I said.

"This park?" asked Roberta.

"Italy," I answered.

"Why?"

"I need to be home."

"And where's that?"

"Dallas."

Roberta gave me a funny look. She disliked Dallas.

"Why Dallas?" she asked.

"I know it sounds funny, but I'm feeling the need to see my parents. I'm also tired of academia. I think I'll be happier in business. I miss making money."

"Advertising?" she asked, knowing I had learned copy-writing during a series of summer jobs.

"Yes."

"But Dallas is sweltering and boring. It's a suburban hell."

"We'll make it work," I promised. "It's filled with possibilities. You'll learn to like it."

Sensing both my desperation and determination, Roberta reluctantly went along with me.

Thus, I became an advertising man with a plan to conquer the world of commerce. The plan didn't work. Boredom got the best of me, and those Ray Charles records I had loved so passionately as a child turned my life in a different direction.

GOD'S
BEHIND
THE
BEAT

Y OU WOULDN'T NORMALLY ASSOCIATE country singer
Willie Nelson with jazz singer Jimmy Scott. Willie is famous, Jimmy hardly known. Willie is a natural-born promoter;
Jimmy, retiring and enigmatic. Both men, I believe, possess genius. Both are unself-consciously daring in their approach to
song, and both have been harshly chastised by critics and colleagues for their unorthodox sense of time. In radical disregard
for conventional phrasing, both sing markedly behind the beat.

No wonder, then, that my collaboration with Willie on his
autobiography, *It's a Long Story: My Life,* got started late. I'd
worked with kicked-back musicians before, but Willie took

it to a new dimension. Days, weeks, or months might pass without a word. But when he did call, his timing was always right. He was ready to entertain my questions. His mood was always mellow. When I started the gig, I worried that I, a marijuana addict with twenty-eight years of sobriety, might relapse. (More about my recovery later.) But I didn't relapse. We didn't discuss pot's addictive properties because, for Willie, those properties don't exist. I wasn't there to reform a man who saw no need for reformation. In fact, Willie was certain that by replacing booze with pot, he had extended his life for decades. I didn't doubt him.

Our conversations took place on his bus traveling from gig to gig, as well as at his sprawling oceanfront home in Maui, Hawaii, and his ranch in the hills outside Austin. I relished those discussions, not only because I got to introduce Willie to the music of Jimmy Scott, which he loved immediately, but also because he indoctrinated me into a new conversational rhythm. Willie said as much with silence as with words. He slowed down the groove without losing its momentum. I found this new beat alluring.

Strangely, Jimmy Scott had me prepared for Willie. Both raised in poverty—Willie in rural poverty, Jimmy in urban poverty—they were lifelong Christians. Their belief in Jesus had survived their hardscrabble and often heartbreaking lives.

Jimmy Scott, the same singer I had heard as a boy when my father delivered pretzels to the Newark bar back in 1953, was championed by Willie's friend Ray Charles. At thirteen, Jimmy saw his mother killed in a car accident at the same time he'd developed Kallmann syndrome, a rare genetic hormonal disorder that impedes growth. He lived his life looking and sounding like a woman. Strangers often called him "ma'am." Small and frail, he was attracted to heavy women who often physically abused him. He said that only his Christian faith kept him from falling into madness.

I called my biography of Jimmy *Faith in Time* not only because his career didn't kick in until late in his life but also because, like Willie, he saw time as an extension of the Holy Spirit.

Jimmy and I did most of our interviews in his house outside Cleveland, where he was raised. He spoke excitedly in a high-pitched voice with a melodious timbre. Sometimes he looked like a lost waif, sometimes he looked like an angel. His brown-skinned face hinted of Native American ancestry.

"People say they're out of time," he said, "but in truth, we have all the time in the world. That's God gift to us. You see, time's infinite. You don't have to understand time in exacting measure. When you sing a song, take all the time you need. Play with time. And, most critically, don't fear time. If you do, time will trip you up. Time is presumed, not achieved. God's the timekeeper. His beating heart provides the rhythm. God's behind the beat. He's behind everything. And like the old saints in church say, just when you think he ain't gonna show up, he shows up—and always right on time."

Jimmy discussed a lifetime of disastrous romantic relationships. His career had proven equally challenging. He started off in the fifties with a big hit sung with vibraphonist Lionel Hampton's band, "Everybody's Somebody's Fool." He recorded with the great jazz modernists, including Charlie Parker, but sales were nil. The big break should have come in the early sixties, when Ray Charles produced and played on a Jimmy Scott album that turned into a grand masterpiece, *Falling in Love Is Wonderful*. But legal wrangles prevented its release. Jimmy was well into his sixties when he met Jeanie, a wolf trainer and, after his mom, the first woman who truly cared for him. It also wasn't until old age that his career was reinvigorated and, instead of working as an orderly or operating an elevator at a downtown Cleveland hotel, he could make records and a modest living singing at clubs.

"I sing behind the beat," he said, "and I live behind the beat. But I tell you, man, I've never lost the beat. I've never lost God."

When we lost Jimmy at age eighty-eight in 2014, I attended the memorial service at the Abyssinian Baptist Church in Harlem, New York. "He sang," I said in my brief eulogy, "as he lived—with great pain and with boundless promise."

MY CONVERSATIONS WITH WILLIE often took place after his marathon poker games held in a spacious room on his Maui property named in honor of the gypsy jazz guitarist Django Reinhardt, one of his major musical influences. It was well past midnight. The moon hung low over the choppy Pacific just feet away. The breezes were mellow, the air sweet, the crashing waves hypnotic.

Because I was intrigued by Willie's notion of elastic time, I questioned him closely about the subject. I read him an Andrew Marvell poem from 1681 that contains the lines "At my back I always hear / time's winged chariot hurrying near." Did Willie ever hear the approach of that chariot?

He smiled and said no. When I told him the title of the poem, "To His Coy Mistress," his smile broadened. "In that case, yes," he added. "When you're trying to bed a woman, you want to hurry up time. But when you're singing a song, you want to stretch it out. And the older you get, the more you understand that time is what you make of it. You can't let it scare you."

On another night at Django's, he had concluded a long series of domino duels and come out ahead. Willie was all smiles. As he began to speak, his voice flowed as naturally as the trade winds. I saw how he expressed only what needed to be expressed. His was a self-editing voice rooted in minimalism. He answered my questions with as few words as possible.

"You believe in reincarnation, although such a belief sits outside traditional Christianity," I said.

"I believe in reincarnation because it's a beautiful belief."

"So you've augmented your Christianity."

"I haven't stayed the same, if that's what you mean. Everyone changes. Jesus was Perfect Man, but Jesus changed. The world changed him. That didn't make him less perfect. Just made him human. So the human and divine live together—least, that's how I see it."

"And is that a comfortable marriage?" I asked.

Willie laughed. "Sometimes yes, sometimes no. But this whole Christian business has gotten way too complicated. The Jews were great about giving us God's law. Jesus was great about giving us God's love. Every religion contains greatness. I just keep going back to Abbott, Texas, and my grandmother, who raised me and my sister, saying,

'Love others like Jesus loves us.' That's where my theology begins and ends."

Studying the clouds blowing over the Maui moon, Willie started talking about Frank Sinatra's version of "Moonlight in Vermont."

"Love his version," said Willie, "and loved Billie Holiday's. Studied the song and realized it didn't contain a single rhyme. That made me love it even more. So I recorded it on my *Stardust* album. Before I put it out, they were saying no country singer should sing those old jazz standards. But *Stardust* sold millions and stayed on the charts for years. I ain't bragging, just saying that a behind-the-beat back-phrasing singer—like Sinatra and Billie phrase—is something that won't ever be going out of style. That's 'cause it relaxes folks to where they think about the story—not just the story of the song but the story of their own lives. You could also say that Jesus's story, in a spiritual way, relaxes us into faith."

BILLIE HOLIDAY'S AUTOBIOGRAPHY, *Lady Sings the Blues*, had relaxed me. I felt like she was talking to me. Because she sang the story of my parents' troubled marriage, because my father had taken me to see her when I was a young boy, and

I heard her mention the name Jimmy Scott, and especially because I played Billie's *Lady in Satin* record for Roberta the first night we met, she remains the artist closest to my heart. I've always sought out people who knew Billie personally. So imagine my surprise when I was told by one of Billie's protégés that, like Willie's and Jimmy's, Billie's sense of song was wed to her sense of divinity.

"No doubt about it," said Carmen McRae, the inventive jazz singer whom I've loved since my father first played her records during my Newark childhood. As an adult, I profiled her for a magazine, and we wound up friends. Carmen was sweet, salty, and uncompromisingly down-to-earth. Richard Pryor cast her as his grandmother—a brothel owner and the most important female figure of his life—in his autobiographical 1986 film *Jo Jo Dancer, Your Life Is Calling.* She had survived the insanely fast-moving world of jazz and worked with everyone from Louis Armstrong, to Noel Coward, to Dave Brubeck.

Carmen invited me to lunch in Beverly Hills, where we ate at the Ginger Man, owned by actor Carroll O'Connor of *All in the Family* fame, a McRae fan (and also a former student of Professor Leslie Fiedler). Carmen ordered a double Scotch and a Caesar salad and started reminiscing about Billie.

"I met her briefly in the late forties," she recalled, "but couldn't really call her a friend until the fifties. She'd ask me over to her place on the West Side, where she spent a lot of time singing the blues about the men who did her wrong. There were many. Then she'd take me to a little Catholic church down the street that was empty except for a couple of old ladies. We'd sit in the back pew, and Billie would get on her knees and cry. I mean, really cry. Tears flowing for five, ten minutes. When she got up to leave, all she said was, 'He heard me. I know he heard me.' That's when I realized that her songs were doing the same thing she was doing in church: reaching out to God. Asking for comfort. Looking for a divine connection, because the human connection—the man-to-woman connection—never worked for her. That's why her music is divine."

ODDLY ENOUGH, I had heard my father say the same thing. I'd introduced him to my close friend Patrick Henderson, a celebrated choir director and composer of sacred songs. At the time, Patrick and I were writing R & B songs, and I invited Dad to one of our sessions. A believing Christian raised in the black Church of God in Christ, Patrick, like Marvin Gaye, was one of first musicians to openly minister to me. He did so with softness and exquisite sensitivity.

"Do you like religious music?" he asked my father.

"If you consider Billie Holiday a religious singer," said Milton, "then I do."

I was shocked. "Religious?" I asked. "You hear Billie as religious?"

"I hear her as mystical," he said, "the way Bach is mystical. You don't have to believe in God to appreciate Billie and Bach, but, listening to them, I'm certain that they did believe in God. Their reverence is what makes their music so moving."

Moving through seven and a half decades of life, I now realize that it is the divinity in music that has sustained me. But in the moment, I couldn't claim that realization. Music moved me, but I couldn't yet name it as the cornerstone of my faith. And one move in particular—from Parma, Italy, to Dallas, Texas—proved as confusing as it was pivotal.

POLYESTER
JUMPSUITS

WHEN I FELT that I was losing my emotional equilibrium in Italy and moved home to Dallas in 1970, my strategy for survival proved effective. Upon arriving in Texas, I did feel reassured by the presence of my parents. They enthusiastically supported my decision to leave academia for business. Both salesmen themselves, they understood that advertising was all about selling and told me what I already knew: that I was good at it. The aspirational energy to move up the economic scale was a deep part of the Ritz family energy, and I was plugging directly into it.

With two friends from college, Richard Cohen and Barry Jagoda, and art director Wayne Houston, I started an ad agency. Our clients included a manufacturer of men's polyester jumpsuits, a national insurance firm, a local spa, a dress designer, a cosmetic line, the Dallas PBS television station, and the Fairmont Hotel. Jagoda, who ran our one-man office in New York, was a brilliant public relations/promo sparkplug who nearly pulled off an American Major League Baseball game in Cuba and a performance of the opera *Aida* in the Houston Astrodome.

Our Dallas office grew to fifteen employees. We weren't getting rich, but we were doing well. I loved dressing the part: Paul Stuart suits, Turnbull & Asser shirts, Ralph Lauren ties, Ferragamo shoes. I liked chasing down new clients and writing ads. Wayne was a wonderful creative collaborator. Richard was the Rock of Gibraltar; a wise and thoughtful consigliere. For a while, we considered venturing beyond advertising and starting a city magazine, but the start-up costs were prohibitive. Then another group launched just such a publication and hired us to both design and promote it.

The birth of *D Magazine* coincided with the birth of our twin daughters, Alison and Jessica. Both births changed my life irrevocably.

I had been ambivalent about having children. Roberta and I had settled into a domestic life with a satisfying rhythm. I organized my records and books alphabetically. On Sunday nights, I lined up the shoes I would wear the coming week and shined them assiduously. I picked out my outfits days in advance. We enjoyed a small circle of friends. Infants were endearing, but they would interrupt my routine. On the other hand, Roberta had no doubts whatsoever. She wanted children, and that was it. I capitulated.

When we learned she was pregnant with twins, we were overjoyed. My resistance collapsed. My hope was for two girls, only because, given my troubled history with Dad, I feared the complexities of father-son entanglements. I figured daughters are more likely to adore, rather than confront, their dads. My wish was granted on September 5, 1974.

I was not prepared for the impact of our daughters' presence in my life. Their preciousness expanded and exposed my heart. I fell deeply in love with them. Watching Roberta breast-feed the babies was moving but left me wanting; I wanted a connection that intimate. Nearly everything about the parenting process pleased me: holding them, changing them, feeding them, comforting them at night when they cried, greeting them in the morning when they awoke. I wanted to be with them all the time.

So did my mother—and, for that matter, my dad. It was the arrival of Alison and Jessica that finally bridged the gap between Mom and Roberta. Until then, Pearl had frozen her out. Now the freeze was melting. Roberta yearned to be as close to my mom as I was to hers, but that wasn't to be. My mother-in-law was incapable of withholding love. I now saw that my mother was extravagantly loving when it came to infants and small children. She was a doting and caring grandmother. I suddenly realized that during a period I was too young to remember, she had treated me similarly. Thus, another gift of fatherhood: seeing Mom loving my children with the same tenderness she had once bestowed upon me.

Motherhood came naturally to Roberta. She handled the twins with marvelous skill. She also made up her mind to return to school: she enrolled at Southern Methodist University, where she became a star student and earned her master's degree in English literature.

THE FIRST ISSUE OF *D MAGAZINE* was hot off the press hours after the babies were born. At first, my role was to simply advertise it. But soon I found myself writing articles. The editors liked my style and asked me to review records and concerts. I wasn't comfortable as a critic, though; I liked praising the music I loved. When I did so, my prose reflected the subject matter and improved. When I wrote negatively about artists who didn't appeal to me, my heart wasn't in it. It wasn't that I was against negative criticism. Critical acumen is essential to everything in life. But when it came to music, my essential interest was celebration. Perhaps it was my inner adman coming out, but I quickly saw celebration as the highest form of criticism.

My journalism expanded beyond music. For *D*, and *Texas Monthly* as well, I expressed my feelings about the wonders of fatherhood. I wrote a lengthy two-part series on the history of the Jews in Dallas. Following the city magazine format, I profiled the ten best lawyers in the region. I profiled jazz musicians and up-and-coming local soul bands. Soul remained on my mind. I was no less passionate about the music of the seventies than I was about the music of the sixties: I was wild for the Jackson 5, Kenny Gamble and Leon Huff's productions of Teddy Pendergrass, the Memphis recordings of Al Green. On the funk front, I embraced it all: the Gap Band, the Average White Band, the Commodores, Chaka Khan and Rufus. When disco hit, I was an unapologetic fan of Donna Summer, Chic, Van McCoy, and the Bee Gees.

My priorities began shifting. I was writing ads and journalism at the same time. In doing so, copywriting felt increasingly shallow and magazine writing increasingly challenging. I had found a form of writing, unlike academic essays or television commercials, where my voice could be expressed naturally. Reading back over these articles now, I squirm at my pretentiousness, but I was moving in the right direction. I was trying to say who I was.

On a personal level, I was trying to do the same. In the

light of gay and women's liberation, seventies culture impacted me deeply. I knew I was heterosexual, but I also knew my homosexual desires had never died. Because the notion of bisexuality was now more acceptable, I could act on it more readily. I wanted to experiment. Roberta and I went into couples therapy, where I argued for an open marriage. Roberta opposed it, but I went ahead with the plan unilaterally. It took me years to realize what had happened, but I now know that my sexual addiction hijacked the experiment. I couldn't regulate my homosexual urges; I acted compulsively. The result was that my recklessness inflicted enormous harm on people close to me. My behavior went on for well over a decade. My behavior nearly destroyed my marriage. I compromised my integrity as a husband. How could Roberta not be furious? She was. I stood in shame. All I could say that I was grateful that Roberta ultimately decided that our union was worth salvaging.

My professional life was as precarious as my personal life. Things were rapidly shifting. My journalism diverted my energy from the ad agency. I no longer cared about chasing after new clients. All I wanted to do was write. Sitting at my IBM Selectric typewriter with its miraculous self-correcting ball of fonts, I was a happy man. I loved not only the act of formulating prose but also the sight of my byline. I had caught a permanent case of writing fever.

By 1976, five years after the agency had begun, I told my partners I wanted out. I was determined to forge a new career as a freelance writer. The dissolution was relatively easy. Everyone understood that I was sincere in my new pursuit. Only my parents had misgivings. They had been heartened by the success of our ad agency and feared for my future. "Freelancing is a tough road," said Dad. "You'll probably wind up writing for a local newspaper, and that won't make you happy."

"Why change directions," asked Mom, "when you have already established yourself? Advertising is a prosperous field. Writing isn't."

Though their admonitions bothered me, I ignored them. Just as I had returned to Dallas for the comfort of being close to my parents, I saw that I now needed distance from them. When I moved back home, they had helped relieve my anxieties. Now they were imposing their own anxieties on me.

There was also the question of our daughters. I wanted to be closer to them. I didn't want to go to an office every day. I wanted to stay home. Thus, another strong appeal of freelance writing. The downside was that my parents' prediction came true.

At age thirty-three, I'd have to write dozens of articles for modest fees in order to make a passable living. I did so, but it was draining; I couldn't see magazine work as a template for my financial future. I'd have to up the ante by writing books. Publishers pay advances. Perhaps I could land a big enough advance to let us live for a while. Roberta pitched in. She became the assistant to Dallas's most prestigious antique dealer. But our combined incomes weren't enough. No way around it, I needed a book deal. That was the moment I decided that, come hell or high water, I'd convince Ray Charles to let me write his life story.

I felt pushed by a groove, but I was still not ready to ascribe that groove to God, much less Jesus. Deep down, I wanted to. It felt good. It felt right. But it also felt like a betrayal. And yet I kept listening to the people I admired most: musicians, whose voices it was my job to channel, even if I hadn't yet fully admitted that those very voices were a conduit for a spirit whose source was divine.

OUTLAW
LADY
AND
DISCO
PREACHER

THE GHOST'S MAIN JOB is listening. Early on, I learned that listening with your ears isn't enough. I had to listen with my heart. If I didn't, the voice I channeled was rendered hollow. Heart listening did not come easy to me. During those times when she emerged from her depression, my mother was a superb listener, but my central role model, my dad, was not. As his son, I wanted to be heard. As a stutterer determined to overcome that challenge, I overtalked. I needed to be recognized and appreciated. But more than any of those things, I needed to succeed. I saw writing as an art form, but I also saw it as a way to make money. *Brother Ray*, my first book, had demonstrated that my primary gift was for ghosting. I soon saw that to make it as a ghost, I'd have to embrace the soul of my collaborator. Locating that soul required listening as I had never listened before.

Because she speaks melodiously, it was easy listening to country singer-songwriter Jessi Colter. Her voice has a beguiling musical lilt. A true-blue daughter of the West—her dad was a miner—Jessi radiates an all-American glow that belies a strong intellect. Her curiosity is keen and her theological background profound. She's a devout Christian. Her mother, Sister Helen, was a Pentecostal preacher who held tent revivals during which Jessi played piano. The family lived in Mesa, Arizona, in an old army barracks that also housed the church, the First Lighthouse Evangelical Center, where Sister Helen presided. As a child, Jessi witnessed miracles. She saw that her mother possessed all the gifts of the spirit. She healed with her hands. She healed with her words. Her fervor for God stilled the angry waters of human rage. Jessi described her as a woman with the power to calm the soul as well as uplift the heart.

For all her biblical devotion and strict reading of Scripture, Sister Helen did not object when her daughter married a rock & roll star, guitar instrumentalist Duane

Eddy—famous for his instrumental hits "Rebel Rouser" and "Peter Gunn"—and began to make records of her own. She further didn't object when Jessi divorced Duane and wed country star Waylon Jennings in 1969. Before Jessi's second marriage, she had begun to question her faith, ingrained in her since childhood, and flirted with New Age philosophies, including the self-centric objectivism of novelist Ayn Rand. When she married Waylon, a musical genius who had rejected his hard-shell Church of God in Christ West Texas upbringing, Jessi found herself drawn back to Jesus.

Jessi didn't do drugs; Waylon did lots of them. Waylon battled with promiscuity; Jessi was faithful. As her faith in God regalvanized, she wondered how to instill such faith in her husband, a man she loved with all her heart. At first, she tried, but Waylon was stubborn, his fundamentalist upbringing still an anathema. Modeling her mother's patience, Jessi waited. Not a month or a year, but decades. She didn't preach, badger, or insist. No well-argued cases for conversion, no sanctimonious edicts. In the end, Waylon saw what he had always seen but was loath to name: the light of God in Jessi's eyes. Before his death in 2002 at age sixty-four, he called that name. He died in peace, saved not by theological argument but the simplicity of pure patience.

Jessi never preached to me. During the many months I spent working with her, I never heard her preach to any of her friends, some of whom were Jewish and Native American. She hung out with poets, philanthropists, painters, and lawyers. Her son, Shooter, is a major musician who works on the avant-garde edge of rootsy Americana rock. Jessi has both written and performed with Shooter, who does not share her fundamentalist Christian faith. Yet she refrains from any attempts at conversion.

We spoke about conversion late one afternoon at the ranch she owns in Scottsdale, Arizona. Decorated in full Western motif, it's a large property set in the midst of the mystical and stark Sonoran Desert. Cacti are scattered across the landscape. Bold rock formations look like modern sculpture. At sunset, the sky turns the world violet. Jessi likes to sit at her grand piano under a huge artwork rendering the Twenty-third Psalm. In fact, she had just completed an album of David's Psalms with producer-guitarist Lenny Kaye, Patti Smith's longtime collaborator.

Jessi formulated sacred-sounding chords as I sat across from her.

"You were raised by a mother who built a career on proselytizing," I said, "and yet you don't believe in proselytizing."

"Sure, I believe in conversion. Jesus's whole ministry

was about trying to convert people from following their own will to following the will of God. But it's all about how you do it," she explained. "Look how he did it. He met people on their terms, not his. The woman at the well. The lepers. His story of the Good Samaritan. If you try to convert anyone without loving him or her first, you'll fail. And since there is no love without compassion—since love *is* compassion—compassion is the key. Compassion doesn't come easy.

"With Waylon," she continued, "I couldn't wait to make him see it my way, live it my way, believe it my way. Part of that was the genuine excitement I felt for the goodness of God, but another part—a huge part—was ego. I had to prevail. So I rushed the process and, in doing so, nearly lost the love of my life."

"What *is* the process?" I asked.

"It's not circumscribed by any law—or even any Scripture—that I know. It's more like music. It has to flow. You follow that flow. The stream might flow to a creek, and a bay might flow to an ocean. You have to trust the flow. Try to control the flow, and you lose God in the process. God is in the flow. God is the flow."

"The groove," I said.

"What we call it isn't as important as how we feel it. We overvalue words. We think they're all we have. But they're restrictive and limiting. Jesus is the living word, but a word best understood and embraced in silence. I believe it's a word embedded in mystery. And the great mysteries remain unsolved. Solve them, and you lose that divine magic."

I CAN'T THINK of a greater contrast in believers than Jessi Colter and Carl Bean. Jessi is a cowgirl country singer. Carl is a gay archbishop and former disco star.

I met Carl through my dear friend actor Dejon Mayes, who invited me to the Unity Fellowship of Christ Church. The membership, drawn largely from Los Angeles's black and Latino LGBT community, was adorned in outfits ranging from fabulously feathered hats to retro pin-striped zoot suits fashioned in fuchsia and forest green. The prelate, Carl Bean, had just delivered a fiery sermon on God's all-inclusive love. The choir had summoned the angels. The congregants had caught the Holy Ghost and celebrated in dance. Spent, I was nonetheless eager to lunch with the archbishop. We went to Roscoe's House of Chicken and Waffles, a close-by after-church spot.

I knew Carl Bean's name from his 1977 Motown hit "I Was Born This Way," among the first openly gay songs in the disco era, but I didn't know his story. A hefty man with a moon-shaped face and soft, dark eyes, he spoke in great bursts of enthusiasm. Sometimes his ideas ran ahead of his excitable voice. He spoke about growing up as a foster child in Baltimore's poorest neighborhood. In 1958, at age fourteen, Carl was a golden boy: an A-plus student, lead singer in the choir, and a precocious student of the Bible. When his foster parents heard neighborhood rumors about his being gay, he admitted it. They recoiled. His foster father beat him. Devastated, Carl swallowed three bottles of pills, but survived, waking up in a Johns Hopkins hospital room, the facility that just happened to be closest to the black ghetto. It was there that Dr. Freund, a woman who spoke in a thick German accent and had come to Baltimore because of Hopkins's progressive reputation, told Carl there was nothing wrong with being gay. She argued against the medical establishment's judgment that termed homosexuality a mental disorder. She explained that this was his sexual nature—and that was that. No need for guilt. No need for regret. The remedy was acceptance.

Carl embraced the remedy. He never looked back. He became an openly gay gospel singer, only to go to secular with "I Was Born This Way." The song's success coincided with the AIDS epidemic, which turned Carl back to his spiritual roots. He devoted his life to issues of gay health and legal rights. Then his activism took on a sacred tone when he founded a church that grew to twenty-five thousand members in twelve cities.

Our lunch was a prelude to starting a book. His story was captivating, but I wanted to get a handle on his message.

"It's simple," he said. "You can't divide God into categories any more than you can divide love into categories. God is love, and love is for everyone. Introduce sexism or racism, homophobia or xenophobia—introduce any form of discrimination, and you destroy the Christian ethos."

I asked him about his witness to the devastation of AIDS. Did it shake his faith?

"It strengthened it," he said. "To watch physical deterioration—slow and horrific—brought me closer to the cross. Without the cross, I wouldn't have made it."

I asked him to elucidate.

"Men died in my arms. Many were skeletal. Some were terrified. Others accepting. But every last one in need of an embrace. A hand to hold. Every last one needed to hear the words 'You are loved. I love you. In all his glory, God loves you.' These were not conversion moments. I did not fear for the souls of these men. My presumption is that we all die to lightness. Darkness is the expression of this world's fears. The requirement was compassion for the human condition at its most vulnerable moment. As I read the story, Jesus expressed doubts. He demonstrated how humanity is built into divinity. He voiced his fears. During the mortification of his flesh, he did not demonstrate perfect faith—I do not believe there is such a thing—but he did demonstrate love even for those who scorned him. So when this world scorns same-sex love, I think of the cross where we were taught that at the maximum moment of fear and pain, it's not only acceptable to cry out, it's righteous and real and ultimately healing. For these long-suffering men, I saw death as the healer. My faith, my imperfect faith, told me that death is not an end but a beginning.

"So you can see how my ability to nurture in the hour of urgent need was rooted in the cross. Death from a frightening disease is the ultimate ordeal. Being with countless others as they faced that ordeal was the most meaningful experience of my life. And viewing that ordeal through the prism of love, no matter how oblique, kept bringing me back to the cross that is, after all, the symbol of triumph over tragedy."

I wondered how Carl ministered to men who considered the disease punishment for being gay.

"I'd say it plainly. God's domain is not over devastating storms that destroy whole populations or diseases that kill babies. God is not a master operator. He's not the Wizard of Oz. He's not a manipulator. Again, his essence is pure love. Because of its purity, God's love is not tainted with punishing toxins. It's a mystical and endless source of positive energy available to anyone humble enough to say 'I'm lonely, I need love. My heart is broken, I need love. I'm afraid, I need love.' Gay love is no different than straight love or bisexual love. It simply is."

I absorbed and believed every word Carl uttered.

STEPPIN'

"IN THE MIDDLE OF LIFE'S JOURNEY," wrote Dante in the famous first line of *The Divine Comedy*, "I found myself in a dark forest where the straight path was lost."

I studied the poem in Italian back in college, but its basic premise—a man seeking a moral compass in middle age—didn't hit me until I entered that very period of my life. I knew I lacked clarity but was adamant about not putting the blame on pot. I loved pot. As a teen, I'd been introduced to pot by jazz musicians, men I revered. Pot represented the culture that molded me: the poetry of Allen Ginsberg and the blues of Ray Charles. Ray and I had gotten high together. Marvin Gaye and I had gotten high together. They had created and recorded and performed high. Following their lead, I had learned to write their books high. Sober revisions were re-

quired, but the initial thrust—the groove that propelled me—
was prompted by pot. And yet . . . say what you want about
pot not being addictive—and I have no doubt that for millions it is not—I was hooked. I'd get high in the mornings,
afternoons, and evenings. Get high to go to the movies. Of
course get high to hear music.

Roberta rebuked me. She saw it was doing me no good.
But my denial was deep. I rationalized that pot moved me in
positive directions. It brought me up. I liked the bump and
the boost. Besides, people I admired lauded it. Willie Nelson saw it as salvation. Marvin Gaye had said, "This violent
world would be more peaceful stoned."

But I was not more peaceful stoned. I was more worked
up, more impulsive, less measured. I was living life through a
haze of marijuana. When Roberta said, "You're using pot to
numb feelings you don't want to feel," I knew she was right
to be alarmed.

Around 1990, I decided to trace those feelings. Maybe even
face them. I tried traditional Freudian analysis. For months, I
submitted to the classic treatment. I was on the couch, the
analyst behind me. Four days a week, we probed the depths.
I liked talking about my mother and father. I liked talking
about myself. I didn't shy away from my complicated sexuality. I looked at my overheated ambition. I discussed my drive.
I examined my fears, the two greatest of which were fear of

failure and fear of death. I droned on, yet after each session, I went to my car and immediately lit the joint that was sitting in the ashtray. Knowing why I was getting high didn't stop me from getting high. I was afraid, and the weed calmed that fear. Weed put a warm filter between me and the cold world. And if weed put things slightly out of focus, I didn't mind. I saw that out-of-focus world as an impressionist painting. So why stop?

Because I was making mistakes. Clarity was clouded. My writing was sounding too shrill or too tentative, too forced or too glib. My hustle was hurting—not slowing down, but mishandled. In pursuing new business, there's a thin line between tenacity and obnoxiousness. I was getting obnoxious, pestering people when I should have chilled. I was giving the impression of desperation when I should I have backed off. Because marijuana cranked me up, I was acting too impetuously too often.

My next move was to leave the psychoanalyst for a narrative psychotherapist. I loved the idea of narrative therapy, which claimed that the way you tell a story impacts the story you are living. Narrative therapy offered me a new approach to my past. I saw that I had been mirroring my father, who, as a young adult, fell into a frozen mythology of his own making. I was caught up in a story that I believed couldn't be changed. But it could. The child caught in the chasm between the bully father and the cold mother might not be caught up in that chasm at all. The chasm might be part of an old story that required major revision, reconstruction, or complete abandonment. Narrative therapy excited me. It also helped me. But it didn't stop me from smoking dope.

Someone said try Alcoholics Anonymous. But booze wasn't my problem. "When they say booze, substitute pot," was the suggestion. I went to a few AA meetings but didn't relate. Then I learned about a twelve-step group for weed. That sounded better.

It *was* better. I heard stories much like my own from men and women who thought they could manage their marijuana intake but wound up stoned all the time. It was important for me to hear other people speak of pot as an insidious addiction. It was equally important for me to identify as an addict. At this point, I simply sought clarity.

I knew little about the origins of twelve-step programs. As I read the basic literature, it didn't take long to learn that it was rooted in evangelical Christianity. That simultaneously bothered me and interested me. It bothered me because they claimed the miraculous basis of recovery was spiritual. I wasn't sure I believed in miracles. It interested me for the same reason Christianity had interested me when visiting black churches as a boy. I saw Christianity as the religion of love. If love was the miraculous aspect of recovery, maybe I could recover.

I was also impressed by how, during the Great Depression,

the founders of this movement, Bill Wilson and Dr. Bob Smith, had radically re-languaged Christian principles to exclude the name of Christ. Had they insisted that recoverers call on the name of Jesus, I would never have signed up. I still wasn't ready. The less specific nomenclature—God—and its euphemism Higher Power—were more acceptable. I still wasn't prepared to answer an old-school altar call. Yet I was ready to listen to the stories of other potheads with struggles similar to mine.

Strange, but it was easier for me to open my heart to them than it was to myself. I had consistently chastised myself for being too weak to quit. When, a decade earlier, I had told Marvin Gaye that I could see myself quitting pot one day, his reply was disparaging: "Once a smoker, always a smoker." I saw it as a matter of discipline and willpower. The program contradicted that, saying it was a matter of willingness. Was I willing to admit that pot had made a mess of my head and that things had gotten out of hand? Was I willing to seek a spiritual—rather than psychoanalytical—solution? Having failed with the first, I was ready to try the second. Was I willing to entertain the notion that a power greater than myself could generate a change in my behavior? And was I willing to turn over my will to that power?

My forays into Christianity had taught me that Jesus's primary mission was to do God's will. So this was straight-up Christianity couched in different terms. The different terms opened the doors to people who, like me, would otherwise balk at declaring Christ Lord and Savior. Yet even without mentioning Jesus, I was doing what millions before me had done: I was asking Jesus to save me.

Jesus. God. Higher Power. What difference did it make? To my forty-seven-year-old Jewish self, not having to publicly embrace Jesus made plenty of difference. I could enter this church of salvation with greater ease. I could attend four or five or six meetings a week and simply listen. I could appreciate the format of those meetings: after I spoke, no one criticized or analyzed or offered advice; everyone just applauded. Whatever I said was sufficient. I could even express skepticism about the program itself. And if I viewed the formal application of the twelve steps themselves as too orthodox, I had only to read the *Big Book* of AA that presented the steps as "suggestions only." Nothing was mandatory. The only requirement for membership was a desire to stop smoking pot. I met the requirement. I joined. And within a few months, I fell in love with the fellowship. I saw how compassion for others led to compassion for myself. The difference between telling a shrink that I was hooked on pot and saying it to a pothead was profound. In the first instance, the secret remained secret. In fact, I was paying a professional obligated to protect my privacy. In the case of the program, I was protected by the anonymity of the meetings. I felt safe speaking whatever was on my mind in a place where raw honesty was honored. The sense of community—one helpless pothead helping another—changed everything.

At first, I complained about the paradoxes. For example, even though recovery was a matter of willingness, it still required willpower to get to meetings, read the literature, and enlist a sponsor. The program might not be based on discipline, but surely discipline played a part. These internal dialogues, though, didn't go on for long. The real-life stories of my fellow potheads took over. I saw them accumulating time away from weed. I saw them healing—all through a program powered by love. I saw them doing what I had convinced myself I could never do: live life without getting high.

January 30, 1990, was the last time I smoked dope. Although booze was never my problem, I gave that up as well, remembering that after a few drinks, the first thing I wanted was a joint. And though from then till now I haven't slipped—no high from any drug—I had yet to face a far more virulent addiction. The truth is that I didn't even consider it an addiction.

I WAS LOST at the midway point of life; still lost in Dante's woods. That's because after I gave up pot, I got hooked on porn and secret sexual liaisons. In dealing with this addiction, I tried to quit the same way I had tried to quit pot: therapy. It was one thing to go a twelve-step meeting and say, "I'm a pothead." But it was another to say, "I'm a sex addict." I didn't want to do that. Yet I couldn't deny that the addiction was dangerous. It was corroding my marriage, not to mention my integrity. No matter, I was not prepared to reveal it to a room of strangers. I returned to the narrative therapist's office, where we discussed the issue and its origins. We concluded that it was a compulsion more insidious than weed. At one point, I committed to the therapist that I would stop my obsessive practice of phone sex with men. I would stop an affair I was having with a woman. I told the therapist he could hold me accountable. Yet he couldn't. I broke my pledge. The secrets remained secrets until Roberta discovered an exorbitant phone bill. That's when I confessed all.

I had wounded her deeply. Yet she did not leave. I thank her for that. But I still couldn't stop. It was only on Yom Kippur, the Jewish High Holy Day of atonement, that things changed. Roberta and our daughters went to synagogue while I stayed home and indulged in phone sex. The next day, I found a twelve-step group that dealt specifically with sex addiction. I was finally able to say the words out loud that I'd been so reluctant to say, even to myself: I was a sex addict.

Back to the program. Back to the twelve steps, which, as I understood, were steps leading to God, the only force capable of resolving the destructive obsession. I had never before discussed my sexuality in an open forum. I knew that anonymity would protect me. My confessions wouldn't leave the room. But I still didn't want to look bad. I still didn't want to tell strangers that I was hooked on porn and engaged in secret liaisons with women and men. Adopting advice given to me from an early sponsor, though, I managed to say the very things I didn't want to say. I took contrary action. I told the truth.

That was twenty-five years ago. Today I remain an active member of that fellowship. The same is not true of twelve-step groups dealing with substance abuse. The desire to drug has long left me. But the urge to act out sexually is alive and well and requires ongoing attention. I continue to attend meetings. I work with sponsors and sponsor others. The program has brought me an uneasy peace of mind.

For a bisexual man to maintain the integrity of a marriage does not require denying his two-sided sexuality, but it does require sacrifice. There are certain things I simply can't do. I can say that I like being straight; I can also say that I like being queer. The cultural and psychological attitudes that accompany both those proclivities are the lenses through which I view the world. I've seen how embracing the truth widens my humanity. If I want to be authentic, and I do, I have no choice but to accept myself as I am.

The relationship between acceptance and indulgence is complex. I am by nature self-indulgent. Give me everything I want, and give it to me now. But what if getting what I want when I want it destroys my integrity and creates familial chaos? What then? I saw that maintaining integrity required a sacrifice possible only with the support of others fighting for their moral sanity—others dealing with their own baffling sexual conflicts. As someone who had written the words "Sexual healing is something that's good for me," I now had to live the life I had written about in the song. The ghost had essentially channeled his own inner voice and now had to find his own groove.

When I considered sacrifice, I considered Jesus. But in my forties, I still wasn't ready. The stubborn and skeptical Jew remained stubborn and skeptical. I still couldn't call myself a Christian and embrace all that I assumed went with that declaration. But I could consider faith. I knew I needed faith.

I found enough faith to entertain the sometimes heartbreaking, sometimes inspiring stories of my program sisters and brothers. Listening to how others struggle with their sexual obsessions engendered my empathy and patience. It also gave me many of the most intimate friendships of my life, each platonic, each appropriate, each rooted in serving each other while staying sexually sober.

Salvation comes through many channels. Just as channeling voice is my livelihood, it also facilitated my recovery. I learned that the voice of the addict dwelling inside me requires attention. The voice has to be heard. The voice says, "Act out! Do what you want! Get what you want and to hell with the consequences!" To mute the voice is impossible. Trying to extinguish the voice only empowers it. The voice relishes struggle. What the voice requires isn't opposition, but understanding. The voice represents part of me, but not all of me. In meetings, I allow that voice to speak without censorship. The voice has things to say that are true. The addict is active and restless and ready to rock. Excavating the shame fueling all that addictive energy is a tricky process. The shame doesn't exist because of homosexual desire. That desire is a precious component of my humanness. It's when the addict hijacks my homosexual desires that chaos ensues. Thus, I act out secretly, compulsively, and self-destructively. My acting out leads to shame that in and of itself is addictive. Voicing the genuineness of my bisexual desires in a climate free of judgment is liberating.

Equally liberating is my willingness to challenge the twelve steps. Program hard-liners take umbrage, but that's okay. Nothing prohibits members from questioning its literature. My questions concern step four, asking that we take a moral inventory; step five, asking that we admit our wrongs; step six, saying we're ready to have "God remove these defects of character"; and step seven, suggesting that we ask "Him to remove our shortcomings." Strict adherence to these steps has surely helped millions of people. The same could be said for any number of spiritual catechisms. But I believe they require scrutiny. With the help of fellow recoverers whose wisdom exceeds mine, I've done deep reconsideration.

As I worked with sponsees, I saw both in them and in myself the tendency to inventory all strictly negative qualities. Doing so unleashed that instinct so many of us share: to beat ourselves up unmercifully. To mitigate that self-defeating pile-on, I found it necessary to inventory positive qualities as well.

I accepted the idea of admitting my wrongs—confession is good for the soul—but realized I also needed to embrace my admirable traits. The inventory required balance. Morever, was I really ready to ask God to remove my defects of character? The first problem is defining a defect. Who's to say? And even if you can nail down a reasonable understanding of your flaws, is God really going to remove them? Experience tells me those failings will never disappear completely. They exist for a reason. Boasting, for example, helps relieve my feelings of inadequacy. Dominating conversations helps assuage my fear of not being heard. The point is to offer compassion to those fears. Learning to live with my defects helps quiet my soul. Praying for their miraculous removal leads to frustration. Defects remain permanent parts of who I am. They can be calibrated up or down. I can arrogantly indulge them or humbly try to soften them. But they ain't disappearing.

Just as Jesus is not cited in the basic literature of twelve-step groups dealing with substance abuse, neither can he be found in the twelve-step material devoted to sex addiction. Yet the more I reflected, the more obvious it was that the program was rooted in the love ethos of Christ. I'd be the last to insist that program members who are Jews, Muslims, Buddhists, Hindus, or even agnostics face that fact. Program members define their Higher Power as they choose. Some atheists, in fact, call the fellowship itself their Higher Power. For me, though, the theological underpinnings of the program drew me back to a specific faith I still had not been able to call my own. I could say I was a pothead. I could say I was a sex addict. But why was I still unable to say I was a Christian?

I can cite all sorts of reasons. My family would not like it. It still felt creepy. Living in America, where Christianity often takes on a tone of xenophobia and right-wing politics, I still harbored prejudice against the religion. Besides, the twelve-step paradigm gave me the freedom to sidestep the thorny issue and define God any way I pleased. Yet that broad definition did not satisfy me. Listening to the jazz masters—Lester Young and Ben Webster, Dexter Gordon and Booker Ervin—listening to the singers—Sarah Vaughan and Dinah Washington, Carmen McRae and Nancy Wilson—listening to the bluesmen—Muddy Waters and Little Walter—listening to the soul stalwarts—Otis Redding and Al Green, David Ruffin and Bobby Womack—and especially listening to the gospel greats—Marvin Winans, Fred Hammond, and Rance Allen, the latter of whom insisted in his mighty collaboration with Kirk Franklin that "Jesus is the sweetest name I know"—listening to these voices that had entered and expanded my soul since I was a kid was more meaningful than ever. They were speaking to me. They were calling me.

"Aretha's father was right," said Reverend James Cleveland, the King of Gospel, when I interviewed him. "Don't matter whether it's Mahalia Jackson or Thelonious Monk. It's all one music. It's all coming from the same place. It's all pointing to the great Creator. It's all God."

EMBRACING THE RIDICULOUS

NTIL HER FINAL DAYS, my mother had little to say about God but a lot to say about clothes. That endeared me to her. We held that passion in common. We both loved to shop at beautiful stores. New season, new colors, artful displays, the continuum of life, the endless optimism of fashion.

Style was the key. As a kid, it was all about Dizzy Gillespie's bebop fashion. I had a Dizzy black beret and, faking an eye exam so I could get glasses, I had a pair of Dizzy's bebop frames with thick black temples. When I was a teen, Miles was the model. This was Davis's Ivy League Brooks Brothers period, and thus it became mine. Blue Oxford shirts with just the right button-down flair. Olive-green sport coats with patch pockets. Outfits that emulated the Modern Jazz Quartet's paisley ties and vested suits. As an adult working in advertising, I indulged my love for English tailoring, especially Egyptian-cotton dress shirts with three-button cuffs and deftly spread collars.

Everything changed when I quit advertising and starting writing books. Again, Miles became the model. Just as he switched musical styles, from bebop, to modal, to fusion, he switched sartorial styles. In an interview, he mentioned his affinity for clothes designer Issey Miyake, whom he called a great artist. Studying some of Miles's Miyake outfits, I understood the trumpeter's meaning. Like Miles, Miyake's fashions were off center and daringly unconventional. He used fabrics the way an artist applies paint or a sculptor manipulates clay. Issey demonstrated that clothes could be art.

In advertising, I chose clothes that, while pleasing my aesthetic, would help my overall sales approach. That required a conservative wardrobe. As a writer, those restraints were removed. My clients were no longer insurance executives. They were artists. That meant wearing artistic clothes that might add to my appeal as I auditioned for the job of ghostly collaborator.

I promised myself that my clothes would not only express my artistic soul but also would be as comfortable as pajamas. That promise led me to Yohji Yamamoto, another Japanese designer who believes in oversized, loose-fitting, flowing garments. As Bird and Diz reigned as my gods of bebop, Issey and Yohji became my sartorial deities. I appreciated how both designers, along with many others I learned to love—Rei Kawakubo, Rick Owens, Ria Dunn, Samuel Ross, Greg Lauren, Uma Wang, Ziggy Chen—wove entertaining threads of irony. Take wrinkles, for example. The old paradigm required that shirts and trousers be ironed to perfection. Wrinkles were the enemy. But free-thinking rebels such as Issey and Yohji said no: wrinkles are fun, wrinkles are intriguing and inevitable, so why not highlight them? The same goes for stains and moth holes and uneven trouser lengths. A lover of funky music, I indulged myself in funky clothes.

It took me a while to accept one of the most obvious facts about funk: that it contains elements of the ridiculous. There's something ridiculous about George Clinton, one of the fathers of funk, stepping off the fake spacecraft "Mothership" with his group Funkadelic in diapers, singing "One Nation Under a Groove." There's something equally ridiculous about wearing a blousy Yamamoto shirt long enough to touch the tops of my shoes. Adding to the ridiculousness is my compulsion to buy every George Clinton record ever released, along with the complete works of everyone from Duke Ellington, to Frank Sinatra, to Prince. Same with clothes. Not one Vivienne Westwood suit but the full fall collection.

I'm not sure how to distinguish an addiction from a fetish, but I do know that both, while serious, are also ridiculous. It's ridiculous to drug your life away. It's ridiculous to undercut your peace of mind with endless pornography. With drugs and sex, I saw where the ridiculous met the lethal. Those addictions could kill me. At the same time, I cling to the rationalization that my two raging addictions, music and clothes, will not kill me. To rationalize even more, I see how they might even help keep me sane. Music makes me feel better about the world and gives voice to my joyful nature. Clothes do much the same, expressing my sense of irrepressible style. And yet the amount of time I devote to music and clothes—falling into two-hour YouTube binges on Merle Haggard and Kendrick Lamar or all-afternoon sessions watching men's fashion shows from Paris online—could surely be called ridiculous.

BACK IN THE EARLY NINETIES, when I was in my late forties, I fell into still another addiction some see as ridiculous: tattoos. The story begins with my children. When

Alison and Jessica were teenagers, they toyed with the idea of getting tattooed. As they leafed through books of various designs, I said, "Maybe I'll get one." They doubted me. They were certain it would never happen. Half to defy them and half to satisfy my curiosity, I went to a tattoo parlor to look around. All I saw were renderings of snarling lions and long-fanged snakes. The clientele was bikers and gangbangers. I quickly left.

"You're right," I told my kids. "I wasn't happy in the tattoo parlor."

That's when Alison handed me a copy of the alternative newspaper *LA Weekly* with a profile of tattooist Jill Jordan, who had been trained at the Otis School of Art and Design and turned down more clients than she accepted. "It's all about the integrity of the tattoo," she told her interviewer.

"She sounds like your kind of person, Daddy," said Jessica.

I went to Jill, who works alone in a nondescript Hollywood apartment, and we hit it off. She was an engaging, openhearted woman with wide-ranging cultural interests and a bohemian vibe. Big band swing was playing on her old-school phonograph. I knew what I wanted: the letters *R & B* on my right arm rendered in a fanciful font and rich colors. Jill said it would take a few weeks to do the design. The weeks passed slowly, but it was worth the wait. I loved the design. Waited another three weeks before Jill had time to actually tat me. I liked the process. The pain was far from excruciating—plus Jill played Big Joe Turner records the entire time.

I thought that would be it. I'd be a middle-aged guy with a small homage to rhythm and blues tattooed on my upper right arm. But what about jazz? I actually fell for jazz before R & B. Why not put *jazz* on my left arm? Jill liked the idea. A month later, I was balanced between two of my favorite genres of music. I thought *that* would be it.

Then came a summer evening when I was seated in New York City's Town Hall, listening to a recital by jazz pianist George Shearing. He was playing "Celia," an exquisite bebop motif of intoxicating twists and turns composed by another pianist, Bud Powell. Mounted on a large wall above Shearing's trio was an oil painting by Stuart Davis, a prominent American modernist who had been deeply influenced by jazz. The painting felt part of the music. The Metropolitan Museum of Art was currently housing a Davis retrospective. Next day, I ran up to the museum and fell in love with Davis's work. I bought a postcard of one of his larger pieces and brought it to Jill, asking whether it might be rendered as a tattoo. She said yes. The rendering, which covered my left arm from wrist to elbow, was perfect. It became my favorite tattoo.

Once I saw that Jill could reimagine abstract art in tattoo forms, the obsession kicked in. A Frank Lloyd Wright stained-glass-window wristband. A geometric Wassily Kandinsky on my right arm. A vibrant Joan Miró on one leg and a splattered Jackson Pollock on another. Over the next six or seven years, the tattoos were added in steady progression— all abstract except the final one, the word *Roberta*.

The tattoo process went on for years. I have no regrets, only satisfaction from viewing them, even today. I don't ascribe great meaning to them. They're not totemic. If they have any symbolic resonance, it's simple joy. They do, I think, echo the rhythms of jazz, but not everyone looking at them feels those rhythms. They're whimsical. I like the idea of permanent whimsy. I like the idea of personalizing my body with splashes of fashion that, again, border on the ridiculous. I learned in Philosophy 101 that the seventeenth-century British philosopher Thomas Hobbes called life "solitary, poor, nasty, brutish, and short." If that's the case, the more ridiculous tattoos, the better.

I wouldn't go so far as to say that my tattoos bonded me to my daughters. They did, though, eventually employ Jill to fashion their own tattoos. Compared with mine, their designs, floral and lyrical, are measured. Alison and Jessica exhibited great restraint, while I threw restraint to the wind.

I like to think our bonding began at birth. It feels like we've always understood one another. I take no credit for the successful women they've become today. Their fierce independence and rigorous discipline seem innate. They are dutiful mothers, loving wives, devoted daughters, and high-achieving professionals: Alison an educator, Jessica a writer. They have benefited from the care of an extremely conscientious mother. They are also funny, unpredictable, and free thinking. Along with Roberta, they have enriched my life and elicited from my heart a kind of overwhelming love I never knew existed.

In 1986, a year before Alison's and Jessica's bat mitzvahs, I interviewed a young woman who, like my daughters, was especially independent and interested in forging a path of her own. She was a singer-songwriter-dancer who'd just released a new album expressing what was on her twenty-year-old mind: *Control*.

SOUL
SISTERS

MY CLOSE FRIENDSHIP with Janet Jackson began when *Essence* magazine asked me to profile her. No longer managed by her father, she had collaborated with the brilliant producers Jimmy Jam and Terry Lewis to create a voice—and a sound—all her own. Her new creed was marked by a celebratory defiance. I grew obsessed with the seductive subtlety of her dance grooves. I loved her songs.

For hours, I watched her perfect the paramilitary moves of a thrilling dance, exhorting the world to break the color line. She was fierce. At the end of the day, I was invited into her trailer, where she had changed from a take-charge black uniform to oversized jeans and loose white T-shirt. She was hardly fierce. She was timid. She also spoke so softly that I strained to hear her. She was uncomfortable being interviewed by a stranger and, with extreme politeness, said the shorter the interview, the better.

Her breakout success seemed a source of embarrassment. Speaking about her private life or professional accomplishments was obviously painful. So instead, we spoke of music—other people's music. Joni Mitchell. Sade. Nina Simone. Janet's spirit awoke at the mention of Marvin Gaye, whom she called "our John Lennon."

She slowly revealed the seriousness of her artistic vision for *Control.* Suddenly her ambition was obvious. In her whisper-quiet way, Janet articulated the grandeur of her artistic dreams. Her confidence, deep and steely strong, was encased in remarkable sweetness.

I was promised twenty minutes but stayed for more than two hours. Eventually the topic turned from music to faith. She sensed that I was a Christian. I wondered why. "Something about you" was all she said. I told her the truth: that I had flirted with Christianity for much of my adult life but never had proposed a formal date. She said that she understood what held me back; there are aspects of all religions that can be off-putting. I asked about her own indoctrination in her mother's religion, Jehovah's Witnesses. Services at Kingdom Hall were mandatory.

Along with her brother Michael, she had accompanied Katherine Jackson door-to-door distributing copies of *Awake!* and *Watchtower* magazines as they sought to sign up lost souls. I wondered if a belief in an imminent apocalypse had unsettled her.

"I'm not sure how deeply I bought into the theology," she said, "as much as I was moved by my mother's devotion. My mother was a force of powerful love, and if this particular faith was adding to that love, I accepted it. For all his faults, I was blessed to have a father who drove his children to succeed and a mother who loved us with all her heart. She also taught us charity. One of the memories I cherish most about Michael was when he and I would buy food and ride around Los Angeles, offering it to the homeless. That was my brother's idea of fun."

I wondered if in leaving her mother's church, she felt as though she were leaving God.

"Never. God is a much bigger idea to me than just one church. In fact, it isn't an idea at all. It isn't what I think. It's what I feel. I feel the presence of God in many things and many ways. A child laughs. A dog barks. The sun sets. The bird takes flight. Sometimes I feel as though there isn't anything *but* God."

As Janet's career progressed, we continued to work together. I wrote more magazine profiles and collaborated on her memoir, *True You: A Journey to Finding and Loving Yourself.* Over the decades, in Tokyo, Sydney, New York, London, and Los Angeles, the dialogue deepened. We wrote about her struggles with low self-esteem, her battles with body image, and the sources of her depression. All the while, her popularity soared to new heights, only to hit a snag and then rebound and gain new momentum.

Her emotional rebound also impressed. Despite a history in which family dysfunction was wounding in the extreme, she always managed to regroup and carry on. Much of this had to do with her loyalty to friends and colleagues. She built up a strong support system. She was also determined to realize her long-held dream of motherhood. That didn't happen until she was fifty. In the wake of the birth of their son, Eissa, she and her husband separated. Difficult legal issues ensued. When I caught up with Janet in 2018, she and Eissa were living in a rented home in Malibu as preparations were under way for a world tour. Pressures, both personal and professional, were intense.

Rather than dwell on the present, we reminisced. I reminded her of all the optimism that undergirded her earlier albums such as *Control* and *Rhythm Nation 1814.* Could that optimism now be sustained? Was the rhythm still right?

"It's still the rhythm that keeps me from getting lost in

the dark places," she reflected. "When I'm not writing or recording or performing, the rhythm can fade, and suddenly time turns sluggish. I genuinely believe there is a rhythm nation that's continually renewed by a younger generation. I also believe that the nation lives inside us as well as outside. Same as God. We get lost. God doesn't. We fall into despair. God eases the fall. Everything we can't accommodate, God can. My mother taught me that God never gives us more than we can handle. She has demonstrated that in her life. In my life, there have been times when I've wondered whether that tenet, though true for Mom, was also true for me. Yet here I am, still ready to get back into the rhythm. I can't speak for others, but what's gotten me through is the goodness of God."

ANOTHER SOUL SISTER, my sibling Elizabeth, six years my junior, had perhaps the most powerful impact on my faith walk. Like Janet, Elizabeth's romantic relationships were difficult. She and her husband, both psychologists, lived in Albuquerque. He was a practicing Catholic who convinced her to cut off ties with her parents and siblings. He considered us dangerously dysfunctional. Ironically, he had no interest in converting Elizabeth, although his religion inevitably became part of her spiritual journey. She felt herself drawn to Catholic sanctuaries, as our mother had been as a child. As children, Elizabeth and I had similar experiences: we both found ourselves intrigued and comforted by Christian churches.

Elizabeth's estrangement from our family was also due to the fact that Milton had told her what he had already told me: that he had a longtime secret lover. After Mom was diagnosed with lung cancer, Elizabeth felt obliged to tell her the truth, writing a letter that exposed our father's betrayal. Mom's reaction was predictable. Pearl lashed out at Milton and threatened to leave. But realizing her need for her husband's care during her health struggle, she stayed. My parents went into couples therapy, though forty years too late.

Everything changed again when my mother called to say "Your sister's marriage has fallen apart." Elizabeth had found the strength to divorce her husband, who moved to the other side of the country, leaving her to care for their three children. In the wake of her divorce, she reestablished close relationships with our mother, father, sister Esther, and me. Her life was in shambles. As a single parent, she needed help. Esther assisted her in writing an ad for a housekeeper, stating that she was seeking a "Christian woman." Esther, who, unlike Elizabeth and me, had not flirted with Christianity, had the sensitivity to understand our sister's needs. That housekeeper turned out to be Rose, who introduced my sister to her policeman husband, Gill. Elizabeth was moved by the extraordinary genuineness with which the couple cared for her children—Gabe, Sarah, and Julia—while she built up her private practice as a psychotherapist. Within a few weeks, Rose and Gill took Elizabeth to an evangelical megachurch, where she experienced a spiritual epiphany. She became a born-again Christian.

"She had an orgasm in church" was how my father cynically phrased it.

Shortly after, my sister called me to explain. She said it was the most illuminating and cataclysmic moment of her life. She now knew God. She now accepted Christ. She had, in fact, experienced a rebirth. She invited me to visit her in Albuquerque, and I accepted immediately. I was skeptical about born-again Christians and especially aggressive proselytizers such as Jews for Jesus. But I also had lived with this unrealized rapport with Jesus for much of my life. Now that my sister had openly embraced Christ, I felt compelled to witness her testimony firsthand. Besides, she had a wonderfully sweet disposition and an extraordinarily compassionate soul. When she had cut off communication with me, I was wounded. Thus, I welcomed our healing and went to Albuquerque with a mixture of glee, apprehension, and curiosity.

Elizabeth *was* changed—there could be no doubt. She was on fire for the Lord. She spoke of him constantly. She had also begun seriously studying the Bible under the tutelage of fundamentalist ministers. I felt drawn to her loving enthusiasm for God but railed against literalism. My reading of the Bible and its history had me believing that human hands—belonging to disciples, scribes, and especially translators—had sculpted and resculpted the text, so that literalism made little sense. As Archbishop Bean pointed out, Jesus hadn't written a word. In the Gospel of John, when Jesus saves the woman accused of adultery from being stoned to death, he uses his finger to write something in the sand, but we don't know what it is. If Jesus wanted his teachings to be followed according to a handbook, he would have crafted that book instead of writing in the shifting sands. The book followed by literalists is one whose canonization and final form is the product of an endless line of scribes with social, political, and theological agendas tied to the times in which they lived and continue to live. The Bible is beautiful; the Bible is deep; the Bible is sacred; the Bible is clear; the Bible is opaque; the Bible is profound, profane, rife with poetry, riddled with contradictions; the Bible is a book and, like all books, subject to interpretation. That means interpretative subjectivity is unavoidable.

Yet as ardently I argued against literalism, I could not argue against the change in Elizabeth's demeanor. She was at peace. With astounding grace, she was weathering the great storm that turned her life upside down. She was also willing to hear me out. She had what I had long wanted: the conviction to say that she believed in Jesus. I also saw in her eyes what I had seen in the eyes of Marvin Gaye before madness clouded his mind: luminous sweetness and gentle peace. Yet I couldn't reconcile that with her adoption of fundamentalism. Our arguments never became strident. We both exhibited patience with each other, but the chasm seemed too wide to bridge.

I went to services at the Albuquerque megachurch where she had been saved. I didn't like it. I thought the preacher was narrow-minded and glib. I told her so, and yet I also said that if this community was giving her comfort, I was all for it.

Back in Los Angeles, I visited similar megachurches, only ones with black congregants, black preachers, and black music. Those were the only sanctuaries where I felt comfortable. If a sermon railed against same-sex relationships, I often walked out. But short of that, the music kept me in my seat or on my feet. The music made me believe that the truth was not in the preaching but in the singing. My gay friends in choirs were equally disturbed by the homophobic ministers yet sang nonetheless. They sang for the same reason I came to church: they found the spirit, unspoiled by bigotry, in the music.

DURING THE WINTER OF 1991, my mother, at age seventy, took a turn for the worse. Cancer had ravished her body. Her last weeks were spent at home in hospice care. My father, two sisters, and I gathered around her bed. We took turns sitting with her. She was in great pain. Her breathing was labored, her coughing incessant, her energy drained. I held her hand and told her that I loved her. "Don't worry," she said, reading my mind. "You can't lose me. I'll always be your mother."

I wanted to offer her words of comfort but had none. No one did except Elizabeth. My younger sister had biblical passages and sacred prayers. Elizabeth felt that our mother was reaching for God and, newly baptized, she was eager to point her in God's direction. Mom gave Elizabeth permission to invite a Jews for Jesus rabbi to our home. Milton threatened to leave the house, but curiosity got the best of him. He stayed. The plan was obvious: Elizabeth wanted my mother to embrace Jesus.

After the rabbi left, I spoke with Mom alone. I reminded myself that of all the people in my life, my mother had always been the most practical-minded and the least likely to believe in far-fetched myths. During her long ordeal, in spite of her physical agony, I did not see her express fear. Though she was stalwart, her essential hardness had softened. I asked her whether all this talk of Jesus was comforting her. She said yes. She said it reminded her of her childhood on Manhattan's Lower East Side when she wandered into Catholic churches.

"Elizabeth is right," she said. "Elizabeth has found what we've all been looking for. Elizabeth has given me what I've always needed."

"And you accept it?" I asked. "You accept God? You accept Jesus?"

"I do. I'm letting go. I'm doing what I've never been able to do. I'm forgiving everyone. Even my father. The burden is lifted. I feel light. I feel God."

I couldn't help but be moved. But another part of me remained skeptical. Wasn't it my mother's extreme vulnerability that allowed her to profess what I had never heard her profess when she was healthy and strong?

Two days later, she died.

I accompanied my father to the crematorium, where we didn't exchange a word. No religious ceremony was held—no preacher or rabbi was called in. But words were spoken when the family came together to sit in a circle and tell stories about the woman who had held us all together. Stories of her determination and strength and salty wisdom. For her part, Elizabeth did not mention the conversion. Tactfully, she did not discuss the transformation that we had witnessed. My father didn't want to hear about it. And neither did I. Now a motherless child, I remained confused and bereft.

My dialogue with Elizabeth intensified as my study of the Bible and Christian theology grew more serious. Still, my sister's fundamentalism continued to disturb me. If that was Christianity, then I wanted nothing to do with it. Of course, I knew there were countless other approaches to biblical understanding, but I found myself stuck in an inane trap of my own making: *I love my sister; she exhibits extreme grace and beauty of character; she comforted our mother at the moment when our mother most needed comfort. And yet I find her version of Christianity naïve and prejudiced.*

My reaction was to research the countless approaches to Jesus that rejected biblical literalism. I studied writers I considered open-minded: C. S. Lewis, Peter Gomes, Marcus Borg, N. T. Wright, Philip Yancey, and Elaine Pagels. I looked at Jesus from the loving points of view of Indian Yogis such as Paramahansa Yogananda and poets like Kahlil Gibran. I read the Gnostic Gospels and the work of the Jesus Seminar, a group of scholars who would spend decades discerning the authenticity of quotations attributed to Jesus.

The more I read, the more I saw fundamentalism as a way to avoid ambiguity and assert certainty. However, my viewpoint was that ambiguity and uncertainty are built into the essential mystery of Christ. When Jesus cries out on the cross, "My God, my God, why hast thou forsaken me?" isn't he uncertain? Yet I wanted to be certain about the corrosive need for certainty; I wanted to be unambiguous about the vital place of ambiguity. I found myself arguing the way my Marxist father had always argued: I had to be right. At the same time, I recognized the necessity of tolerance. And so did Elizabeth. Thus, we tolerated each other's intolerance.

Matters became more muddled when Elizabeth's daughter Sarah, then a teenager, exhibited dangerous self-destructive behavior. This was after my niece had gone to live with her father for six months and Elizabeth had put her into therapy. Sarah kept spiraling down. With great sorrow, Elizabeth's solution was to forcibly send Sarah to the Holy Highway Girls Home in rural Texas. After Sarah was there for several months, I accompanied Elizabeth on a visit. The Christian vibe was undiluted fundamentalism. Additionally, the girls were given rigorous daily chores, including farm duties. I attended services led by the ebullient school leader Sister Janis and, despite my initial reservations, felt drawn to her loving energy. On the day that Sarah graduated, Elizabeth, my father, and I attended the ceremony. When Sarah spoke of her gratitude for the school and her salvation, we were all moved to tears, including Milton. I asked my niece, now completely transformed, to what she ascribed her miraculous change, and her answer was "Jesus."

Still struggling with single motherhood, Elizabeth felt the need to leave New Mexico and move her family to Dallas. Dad, who had a modest three-bedroom duplex there, took in Elizabeth and his granddaughters for six months, while Gabe went off to college. At eighty-one, he had retired and was enjoying his leisurely life of listening to music and attending a monthly philosophy forum at which he debated heavyweight academics. He spent a year preparing a paper on the prominent Hungarian-British writer Arthur Koestler, described as an intellectual and sexual adventurer. I flew to Dallas, where Elizabeth and I heard Dad deliver his ninety-minute lecture.

My father's phenomenal dedication to Elizabeth and her children was inspiring. He was willing to disrupt his otherwise orderly life. He grocery shopped, cleaned the house, and drove his granddaughter Julia to high school. He also watched Elizabeth join an ultrafundamentalist megachurch, which then hired her as a psychologist. I attended several services with her and met her supervisor. For me, it was all too big, too slick, too programmed. I didn't like my sister's boss and was skeptical of the bureaucratic hierarchy in which he enjoyed prominence. It was a weird juncture where

American Bible-centric Christianity married American corporate capitalism. Yet I saw how Elizabeth tried to do her work diligently and lovingly, and I supported her efforts.

Flying in from Los Angeles every few months, I sat around Dad's dining room table, where the theological disputations were endless. Seeing that his younger daughter had embraced Christianity and his son was studying it disturbed him. He was eager for verbal battle. Like me, he loved Elizabeth dearly and had taken extraordinary measures to help her through single parenthood. Also like me, he had qualms with her theological alignment. These were difficult discussions. I wanted to defend Jesus and defy my father's atheism. He couched everything in terms of "liberal humanism": a world of love, he called it, without God. I argued that God *was* love. At the same time, if Jesus was the God of love, how could Elizabeth abide the unloving intolerance of her teachers who insisted that the holy book be followed as if its inconsistencies and contradictory messages were nonexistent? Yet these were the teachers who had seen my sister through the storm of her domestic life, galvanized her faith, and saved her daughter.

Even as inconsistencies and contradictions resonated in the Bible, they resonated even more blatantly inside my own head. I was bewildered.

SILLY
INSISTENCE

NATALIE COLE HAD ALREADY WRITTEN a full-length autobiography. She hired me to ghost her book about an improbable confluence of events, simultaneously tragic and triumphant. In 2009, as Natalie's sister Carole "Cooke" Cole was dying from lung cancer, Natalie would also have died without a new kidney. She had to leave Cooke's bedside to undergo a transplant operation. It was the death of Jessica Karina, sister of Patty Argueta, both complete strangers to Natalie, that facilitated the miracle. Natalie successfully received Jessica's kidney. Eventually Natalie sought out and befriended the young donor's family.

Natalie saw the story as a confirmation of faith, not because she had survived and her sister had not, but because of her connection with Patty Argueta. As she lost one sister, she gained another. At Cooke's memorial service, Natalie studied her sister's photograph under which was written, "Be still and know that I am."

"For all their ambiguity," said Natalie, "those were the words that sustained me."

Five years later, just before Natalie herself entered the hospital, she phoned me. It was our last conversation.

Having been converted to evangelical Christianity in Chicago by her aunt Bay, who lived in the projects and ran a beauty salon, Natalie wanted to be make sure Bay's name would not be forgotten.

"When I was strung out on heroin," she said, "it was Bay who took me in. I kept staring at the plastic plaque on Bay's living room window that said 'Expect a miracle.' Bay was my miracle. I already was something of a star, but Bay saw my star falling. She pointed me to another star, the only real star. Church became my salvation. The twelve steps were the practical means to maintain that salvation. Those steps led me to Bay's star. Like Bay, I called the star Jesus, but Cooke didn't. Cooke was a New Age spiritual searcher, a hippie, an actress, a bold individualist. She and I would have long talks about the name of God, about my insistence on calling him Jesus. But now when I think about those words under her photo—'Be still and know that I am'—I'm convinced that our love came from the same source. For some people, like my precious sister Cooke, that's enough. For me, though, I love the name Jesus. I still hear Aunt Bay saying that name. The name is music to my ears."

Five weeks later, Natalie died of congestive heart failure. She was sixty-five.

NATALIE WAS RAISED in the same general neighborhood of Los Angeles where both Tavis Smiley and I lived. Before I met either of them, I had watched Tavis interview the singer on his PBS broadcast. They both were slain by the spirit in Pentecostal churches.

Tavis was twelve when he and his sister were chastised from the pulpit of the family Pentecostal congregation in Kokomo, Indiana. His parents, both church elders, were seated in the front pew next to their children. The preacher's harsh accusations of miscreant behavior were based on false information, but Tavis's father took them at face value. That afternoon, he unmercifully beat Tavis and his sister to where they required hospitalization. Upon release, Tavis chose not to return home but to live with foster parents for five long months.

Tavis and I would eventually write four books together: his autobiography, as well as reflections on Dr. Martin Luther

King Jr., Maya Angelou, and Michael Jackson. But nothing in our work impressed me more than the story of his beating. When he described the incident, his eyes were moist. His usually confident voice was shaken. He called it the lowest point in his life. When he finally moved back home, his parents refused to help him realize his ambition to attend college. Tavis simply showed up at Indiana University and talked a dean into providing financial aid.

Yet, as an adult, Tavis was the most devoted son I knew— and also a devoted Christian. For days, we sat in my home study as he painstakingly explained his coming to terms with his past. Surprisingly, he used words similar to the words Natalie had used.

"Insisting on being right is silly," he said. "Kids are silly, and I was no different. The injustice I suffered was terribly painful. The humiliation was even worse than the physical pain. I'm not calling that silly. What's silly—and, even worse, counterproductive—is to use that injustice against yourself. To hold on to it like a weapon to strike someone else. Or use that weapon to inflict self-harm. Instead, I used that incident to drive me forward. I used it to show the world that I could do something, that I was worth something, and that I could achieve beyond the limited expectations set up by my childhood. Being raised in a trailer with ten siblings in small-town Indiana could limit anyone's expectations."

"But what expanded those expectations?" I asked.

"God. Jesus. The Holy Ghost rained down on me. That shower of love was nothing I could deny. It was something I felt. I love James Taylor's song 'Shower the People' because it puts me in the same place. Truth is, for all that happened to me in childhood, I still attend a Pentecostal church because of its spirit. That spirit transcends all aggressions. It gets me up and keeps me going. In its essence, it's a spirit free of negativity. It's the spirit you hear in the music. That's the spirit that led me to forgive my father, forgive and love him, knowing that his limitations, like mine, are part of his imperfect humanity."

Tavis got me thinking of my own father, who was approaching ninety. Had I simply tolerated him or had I actually forgiven him? I mouthed the clichés—that he'd done the best he could—but that was different from real reconciliation. Was I capable of showering him with love?

It also got me to thinking of the very thing I'd been considering for decades: going ahead and calling myself a Christian. How long would the fear of that simple statement continue to haunt me?

GLORY
IN
THE
STORY

T HE GOD THING, the Jesus thing, the whole spiritual apparatus was something I saw as a cloud floating above me. It was ethereal. It was porous. It was beautiful. It changed shapes, it appeared and disappeared, it was filled with light, but was it real? How I could concretize it? How could I embrace it? How could I keep it from dissipating into the atmosphere?

To answer those questions, I had three resources: I could listen to music about God, I could read about God, and I could write about God. I did all three compulsively. Music was the most important because it was the most immediate.

It was emotional rather than intellectual. But I couldn't fool myself: as the son of a deep thinker, I was incapable of completely abandoning an intellectual approach to God.

Eventually, reading about Christianity wore me out. The reading was fascinating, but the motive behind it—to get myself to believe through faultless reasoning and logic—was not productive. The authors and their arguments rattled inside my head. Headaches were followed by depression; depression, by despair. I wasn't sure that I'd ever figure out this thing. Some churches, with their jubilant music, satisfied my emotional needs. Some, with enlightened preaching, satisfied my mind. But I never found a church that did both. In Episcopal sanctuaries, I liked the progressive thought but was bored by the traditional English hymns. In black churches, the choirs stirred my soul, but the sermons didn't always satisfy.

I was in my late fifties when three phenomena helped resolve my dilemma. The first was a record by a friend, Howard Hewett, who had been the lead singer of the popular R & B group Shalamar. He had forged a solo career and, in doing so, cut a spiritual album, *The Journey*, in 2001. I had always been drawn to the searing beauty of Howard's high tenor, but this suite of songs, like Marvin Gaye's *What's Going On*, had me half crazed. I couldn't stop listening to it. It's basically the testimony of Howard's faith in Christ, but his way of telling the story—his paradigm of the circuitous path to God—resonated. Circuitousness was okay. Doubt was okay. Without doubt, there is no faith. Faith doesn't remove doubt; it simply allows us to live with doubt without going mad. For months, I meditated on Howard's music. I went on his *Journey* and, as a result, felt myself changing.

The second change came from another dear friend, Mable John. I had met her thirty years earlier, when she was the lead Raelette, a Ray Charles background vocalist. She and Ray were close. Her brother was the remarkable R & B singer Little Willie John, who had greatly influenced Marvin Gaye. Earlier, Mable had enjoyed a solo career as the first female singer on Motown and an artist on the famed Stax label, whose sixties soul sound remains one of the great glories of American music. One night, while singing with Ray, an inner voice told her, "Go home." She interpreted the voice both figuratively and literally. She left the tour and came home to Los Angeles to study for the ministry.

Rather than buy or build a church, she conducted Sunday services in her lovely home, only a few miles from mine. The services were simple. Occasionally there was a piano player. Her son played bass. Nine or ten of us sat in chairs and sofas in her living room. On the wall hung a photograph of Mable and Billie Holiday as young women at the Flame Show Bar in Detroit in the fifties. It was meaningful that Billie, even as a photographic image, was present. Songs were sung, prayers offered, but mainly Mable spoke. She spoke simply and directly, just as she had spoken simply and directly to me for all the years I had known and loved her. Thirteen years my senior, she was a woman who displayed deep sincerity, easy humor, and undying passion for God. The God she loved went by the name of Jesus, and to hear her say that name always thrilled me. But unlike many male preachers I had heard, Mable didn't invoke the name for its thunderous effect. She didn't exploit the inherent drama of the name to boost her prowess as a preacher. She spoke of Jesus as if she knew him. She spoke of Jesus as though he loved her. And she spoke of that love as the most natural thing in the world. That love required no analysis, no critiques, no complex delineations. The love was simply there on display in Mable's heart. She explained further that it was a love available to all, a love that excluded no one, a love that required only recognition and acceptance.

While I was attending services at Mable's home, I was also invited to a men's group that met weekly to discuss their conscious contact with God—or lack thereof. Some of the participants were twelve-steppers, but many were not. A half dozen in number, we took turns speaking. There was no format or text. The informal leaders, Ed Lassiter and Skip Smith, decided that the less structure, the freer the spirit to inform. Ed and Skip were Christians, but several of the men were not. God was the topic, but not God as an abstract idea; God as a comfort in our daily lives. Our stories concerned those times when we could access that comfort and those times when we couldn't. Far more stories described our separation from God than our connection. An engineer and entrepreneur, Ed seemed to be a man whose connection was visible and constant. His faith impressed me.

Howard Hewett's healing Marvin Gaye–informed gospel music; a soft and humble woman minister; a group of men discussing the power of God without I-have-to-be-right rancor; and my deepening commitment to the Higher Power I'd learned to love in twenty-one years of twelve-step meetings—they all fused in my heart.

I MET FREQUENTLY with Bishop Noel Jones, the man I call the John Coltrane of preachers. We'd become friends. Noel, the brother of singer Grace Jones, leads the City of Refuge, a black megachurch just south of LA. His sermons reminded me of the great jazz saxophonist because they were spontaneous sheets of sound filled with spiritual surprise. Noel had suffered under the tutelage of a strict apostolic preacher father yet became a minister himself, adopting the Pentecostal style of sermonizing while imbuing it with progressive ideas. As a storyteller, he was spellbinding. Just as I never tired of Coltrane's endless variations on "A Love Supreme," I never tired of Noel's eloquent riffs on the centrality of Christ.

I came to his home in a neighborhood close to Los Angeles International Airport and sat in his study, where we listened to jazz and discussed the deep issues. A man of the cloth, he was also a man of the world. He'd gone through a divorce. He'd enjoyed the material comforts of being a superstar in the world of black Christianity. He liked fine wine, fine dining, elegant clothes. He was acutely aware of the irony of being affluent while serving a God who, during his time on earth, was homeless. He had reservations about the gospel of prosperity, so popular among many of his colleagues. He was open about his conflicts. He was self-aware and highly self-critical. I loved Noel, especially when he talked about the purpose of pain.

"We're broken," he said. "That's our condition. We try and we fail. We aspire and we fall. We do all we can to perfect our love that, as long as we live, will remain imperfect. But here's the beautiful part; here's the part that keeps me going, the part that lights the way: God uses our brokenness. He uses our defeats. He uses our pain. He uses our flaws and frustrations to bring us to him. The pain is the path.

"Take the Lazarus story. Jesus loves the little family of

Lazarus and his sisters, Mary and Martha. But when he hears Lazarus is dying, he waits two days before attending to him. By then, the brother is gone. The sisters are frantic, crying out to the Master, 'If you'd only been on time, Lazarus would have lived.' What's happening here? God is using the sisters' pain to bring them closer to him. He's creating a situation that will yield a revelation. He's inserting himself into the family's story to focus on the Father. So his words about the brother, 'Unbind him, loose him, let him go,' are words for us: *unbind ourselves, loose ourselves, let ourselves go.* He gives fresh life to Lazarus. He gives fresh life to us. But that freshness comes through pain, a freshness born out of frustration and finally reconciled in faith. I'm not saying that when pain is present we can jump with joy. But we can stay steady, knowing that the sacred storyteller is in full command. And the story ends, begins, and is always bathed in glory."

AL GREEN SANG A SONG called "Take Me to the River," a muddy mix of earthly love gone bad only to be salvaged by the holy water of baptism. I'd been listening to the song for years. When Noel Jones used the phrase "bathed in glory," I thought about the river. The thought gave rise to a voice inside my head that said clearly, "I want to be baptized."

I wanted to make a public declaration. It was important to me that my profession be heard by those closest to me. I no longer wanted it to linger as a half secret. If I carried any weight of guilt or shame for being a Jew who loved Jesus, I wanted to put down that burden.

Yet I confess that the decision alarmed me. I was frightened, in part, because I worried it would alarm my wife, my children—then in their early thirties—and my dad, then eighty-eight. I remembered the huge family trauma that had resulted after my sister Elizabeth's conversion. I wanted to avoid such a trauma. I also wanted to avoid being labeled a born-again Jew or a Jew for Jesus because I saw them, fairly or not, as literalists and proselytizers. I was neither. I had no interest in converting anyone. I had a hard enough time converting myself. So I was afraid of being labeled. I was afraid of being misunderstood. I was afraid of being judged. I was afraid of having to defend Christianity against those whose viewed Christianity as an expression of right-wing fundamentalists. I was afraid that my close friends, most of whom are not Christian, would condemn me as a fanatic. I envisioned having to explain and justify my faith for the rest of my life. In short, I leaped out of the present and into the future, where fear loves to lurk.

Theology continued to plague me. These were mighty internal intellectual battles. The nature of the Trinity. The paradox of Christ's dual divinity/humanity. Was Jesus an absolutist or a revolutionary fighting absolutists? And why no word from the Son of God about the evils of slavery during his time on earth? And were the miracles actual or metaphorical? Did they need to be expurgated, as Thomas Jefferson had done in his redaction of the Bible, to dispel the hocus-pocus and highlight the purity of Jesus's message?

I embraced certain concepts without equivocation. Grace, for instance. I loved the notion of grace: that we don't earn God's love; we are gifted God's love. I loved the notion of radical forgiveness. But mainly I loved the name Jesus. That had nothing to do with theology. It had everything to do with the name. To resist this sound was nothing short of hypocrisy. To be honest with myself, I'd have to put aside theology and say simply "I love the name Jesus. I love Jesus."

But what does that mean? Doesn't my declaration of faith require an accompanying treatise explaining which Christian doctrines I accept and which I reject? Don't I need to write it all out, appear before an official committee, submit myself to rigorous questioning, and hope for approval?

Hearing these questions, Mable John simply smiled her sweet smile and said, "David, I know you love the Lord. His love comes through you so loud and strong that everyone feels it. Even our friend Ray Charles can see it. Now, if you want to publicly say you love him and go under the water, I'll stand by your side. But I'm not pushing you. The only one doing the pushing is Jesus."

My decision to go under the water and be baptized, with Mable by my side, was ultimately easy. When the debate inside my head finally quieted, it became obvious. This was my heart's desire. At sixty, I thought back to my bar mitzvah forty-seven years earlier. I did not feel then that I had connected to a mystical and endless source of love. I did not feel much of anything. But now, at this moment in my life, I wanted to experience a different kind of bar mitzvah, one filled with emotional meaning. I was ready to declare my love of God. That declaration felt neither rebellious nor obligatory. It simply felt good. It felt even better when I learned that the church Mable was using for the baptism was a former Jewish synagogue that had been converted to a black Baptist sanctuary in an African American neighborhood in Inglewood, California.

JULY 25, 2004

I INVITED DOZENS OF MY FRIENDS and, of course, my family. My dad was the most challenging invitee of all. That's because in the many years since my sister Elizabeth had converted, he saw me as his ally. Now I was deserting him. We argued like crazy about God. He clung to what seemed to me his inbred Marxist skepticism. But he had always been comforted by the fact that, unlike Elizabeth, I was not calling myself a Christian. Now all that would change.

When I told Milton my decision to be baptized, the conversation was surprisingly short. His first words were: "I think you're crazy."

A long pause followed. I pledged not to defend myself and get into a pointless argument. I stayed silent until he added, "But I'm coming."

"You're flying in from Dallas?"

"I have to," he said. "I have to show you unconditional love."

Like nothing my father had ever said to me before, his words warmed my heart.

Thus, my dad and sister Elizabeth arrived together, along with my wife, who was understandably upset about the whole thing. Roberta sat next to my dear friend Harry Weinger, a soul music scholar/high-ranking executive for Universal Records, who reported that she was ashen and in tears for most of the service. She was afraid that I'd become a fanatic. I understood. I also understood why my daughters decided not to attend—not in protest, but because, I believe, they were still a little bewildered. At the same time, they accepted my decision without argument. My friends,

Jewish and non-Jewish, showed up. Janet Jackson was kind enough to attend. Howard Hewett sang portions of *The Journey*. I could not have asked for a greater blessing. Wearing a white robe, I shared the day with several other baptismal candidates and went under the water. Doubts disappeared. I don't mean doubts about theology; I'm prepared to live with those doubts forever. The formula that comforted me was: *no doubt, no faith*. The doubts that vanished were about whether I had done the right thing. I knew I had.

It took a while for things to settle down in my immediate family. I think my wife and daughters were waiting to see whether I'd try to bring them into the fold. When they saw I had no interest in converting anyone, they relaxed.

As the years went by, I thought long and hard about what it means to profess one's faith and make it meaningful. At thirteen, I had tried do so with my bar mitzvah and failed. At sixty, I had tried to do so with my baptism and succeeded. That's because my second attempt was fueled by authenticity of feeling, not social obligation. I authentically felt that I was—and wanted to call myself—a Christian. It did not mean that I was denouncing my Judaism. Even now, if someone asks me if I'm Jewish, I answer yes. I like being Jewish. I've always liked being Jewish. At the same time, if someone asks me if I'm Christian, I also say yes. In my heart, the two are inseparable. Without one, the other doesn't exist.

In the simplest terms—the terms that quieted the raucous arguments inside my head—Judaism laid down the law, and Christianity tempered that law with love.

Why is it, though, some Christian friends ask me, that I don't feel obligated or even moved to convince my family and friends to follow me down this path? The reason is simple: as a follower of Christ, my role is to spread love, not insist on specific nomenclature.

I LOVED MY FATHER as much as I have ever loved anyone. He cared for his children. He cared for his grandchildren. In his own messed-up way, he cared for his wife, and he cared for his girlfriend. He taught me to love jazz and books. He taught me to challenge authority and to value critical acumen. He was funny and kind and charismatic and larger than life. But for all his goodness, he never learned to listen. His mission was to prove himself. He wanted to—he needed to—listen to himself more than he wanted to listen to anyone else. My essential lesson was that loving him no longer meant pleasing him, especially in matters as critical as religious belief. Rather than emulate him, I had to separate myself from him. He didn't believe. I did. Ironically, for that separation to prove successful, I needed to have more compassion for him. To be free of his injurious example, I had to love him even more.

One manifestation of that love was to invite him on a trip back to New York City for his ninetieth birthday in 2006, just the two of us. I insisted we fly first class. He said I was being indulgent. I said he was right, but I was paying. Once we got on the plane and he saw empty seats in the coach section, he urged me to take those seats and get a refund. I said it didn't work that way. On the flight, he read Saul Bellow's last novel, *Ravelstein*, about the death of an intellectual, while I read August Wilson's *Fences* and resonated with the line "Your daddy wanted you to be everything he wasn't . . . and at the same time, he tried to make you into everything he was."

I booked a suite in a hotel Milton thought too luxurious, but he finally surrendered to the spectacular view of the Chrysler Building. He was animated and energetic and amazingly youthful for his age. I arranged lunches with several of my editors, whom he charmed with his erudition and wit. He exaggerated, he boasted, he dominated, but it no longer mattered. I was proud of his ninety-year-old vitality. I didn't resist. I let him rant. I took him to meet my beloved literary agent, David Vigliano, whose office on Lower Broadway turned out to be in the same building and on the very same floor of the former hat factory where, sixty-six years earlier, my father had met my mother. Will the circle be unbroken?

We drove to Newark to revisit Dad's old haunts and then to Dover, New Jersey, to see his closest friend, Lil Loewenthal, a biographer of modern dancer Isadora Duncan. Back in the city, we heard vocalist Shirley Horn, whose whisper-quiet styling echoed the last years in the life of Billie Holiday, my parents' favorite singer and the sacred seductress who first lured me into the misty blue world of jazz.

We wandered through the Museum of Modern Art to revisit the Monets that he and Mom had introduced me to when I was a child. On the Lower East Side, we ate pastrami at Katz's Deli and knishes at the Yonah Schimmel Bakery before heading over to the Strand bookstore, where Dad once bought me a copy of Henry Roth's *Call It Sleep*, an epic novel from the thirties about growing up in the Jewish ghettoes of New York City.

During this prolonged and overdue father-son celebration, we didn't argue once. He accepted me. I accepted him. I said that I was grateful that he was my father. He said I had made him proud. Reconciliation finally realized.

MILTON RITZ LIVED another five years, the last two in assisted living. He remained coherent to the end. Impatience did him in. Rather than wait for the orderlies to help escort him to dinner—they were five minutes late—he decided to walk to the dining room. He fell and never got up. My sisters, Esther and Elizabeth, and I were with him the last two weeks of his life when he was confined to a hospital bed. No conversion was attempted. We knew better. I brought in a boom box and played the classical and jazz music he loved most. He went out in a coma. I thought we had closure. I thought I was prepared for his death.

I wasn't. I needed to get in touch with him and didn't know how. I didn't understand life without him. I felt on the verge of losing it. Couldn't sleep. Suffered anxiety attacks. Sought professional help. I prayed. I considered doing drugs, acting out sexually—anything to assuage the fear. Finally, I saw that all I could do was walk through the fear. But on the other side was more fear. I wanted my daddy, who had always protected me, and now my daddy was gone. At last, the fear quieted, but only because I followed the advice of the bluesman who'd said, "You sing the blues to lose the blues." Only when I wrote about my father at great length did the blues start to lift. I wrote him letters, keeping him abreast of the Dallas Cowboys and describing the latest Philip Roth novel.

AGING GHOST, ENDLESS GROOVE

T O BE OF LITERARY SERVICE is a rare gift. I think of the 1998 movie *Central Station*, in which the Brazilian actress Fernanda Montenegro plays a schoolteacher who, standing in front of Rio de Janeiro's main train station, helps illiterate passengers compose postcards. I see myself in a somewhat similar position.

Had I fulfilled earlier dreams inherited from my father of becoming a bombastic critic such as Leslie Fiedler or an acclaimed novelist like Bernard Malamud, my ego would have eaten me alive. Ghosting has kept my ego at bay. To be a good ghost—and to maintain a comfortable lifestyle—has meant putting other people's stories before mine. Were it not a professional mandate, I'm not sure I'd ever get over myself. Ultimately, getting over myself has meant getting to God.

The joy I derive from writing is visceral. It has much to do with the physical act of typing. I love to type. I loved the old-school Underwoods and Remingtons, with their imposing weight, moving bars, and ever-satisfying bells; loved pounding the keys and watching them attack the page; loved the electrics that afforded me lightning speed; loved the IBM Selectric, with its spinning ball and self-correcting key; loved how computers—starting with the portable Kaypros and running through the iMacs—essentially kept the same keyboard figuration, thus allowing me to gain even greater speed while, miracle of miracles, editing electronically. As much as I got a kick out of typing as a kid, computer typing brings me even greater joy, especially because a world of endless research is available at my fingertips.

Beyond the fun of typing—the *click-click-click* of positive productivity—there is the analogy between my craft and my mother's. An expert seamstress, she spent hours at her sewing machine. As a young boy, I marveled at her dexterity and wondered if I could ever develop the patience to sit and single-mindedly pursue such a craft. As a worker, she is my model. So are shoemakers and carpenters. As a writer, my first job is to construct a sturdy story.

I've avoided writer's block, I believe, because I remember not to take writing all that seriously. Which isn't to say I'm not a serious writer. I'm just not dead serious. I like most of the books I've written. Many I even love. But I see them for what they are: human stories that may or not interest you. I had to shed the somberness of my English major education that never—not once—presented literature as light or even frivolous entertainment. Literature was Dante, Shakespeare, and Proust. Literature was high art whose creation demanded genius.

Leslie Fiedler argued for the validity of pop culture, but he did so in the dazzlingly intellectual lexicon of the high-minded critics he sought to undermine. When I told him I had become a ghostwriter, he wasn't displeased, but perplexed. I had to explain the job to him.

My on-the-job training taught me that sculpting someone else's story is tricky business. Sometimes I could create a true likeness; sometimes I couldn't. In the end, though, the process has been both the challenge and the reward. Of my some five dozen books, five have landed on bestseller lists, six have won awards, and the others exist in various degrees of obscurity. I don't mind. I enjoyed the typing, enjoyed the writing, and even learned to enjoy the relief of impermanence. A book is a beautiful thing, but so is a flower that wilts or a pair of sneakers that wears thin.

For me, the pleasure in writing is finding the groove: the

rhythm that organizes time into intoxicating syncopation, the enchantment that comes with free improvisation, the comfort of a steady beat.

That beat is holy.

"Does it have a good beat?" was the question kids of my generation were asked about a new song by Chuck Berry or Little Richard.

The answer was yes.

To get to the heart of that beat—the heart of the story, the creative process, the mystical nature of the divine—is to keep dancing, keep trucking, keep writing. I accomplish that by having fun. My office is filled with dozens of dolls, stuffed animals, and bobbleheads of everyone from Dodgers baseball announcer Vin Scully to Jesus. They remind me to be playful. I want to play in the sense that Oscar Peterson and Herbie Hancock play piano. The computer keyboard is my instrument. It's an instrument of pleasure. I see the computer as a toy. I'm messing around, fooling around, running around in a playground where storytelling is a game.

I'M HAPPY TO BE OLD. Happy to be seventy-five. Happy to be alive at a time when "Loyalty," Kendrick Lamar's rap with Rihanna, has me thinking back to "My Sweet Hunk O' Trash," the Louis Armstrong–Billie Holiday duet recorded nearly seven decades earlier. The music that has sustained me since childhood sustains me still. I have aged, but the music has not. The music sounds better than ever. Hour after hour, I inundate myself, via Spotify, with dozens of versions of "Body and Soul," from Dexter Gordon to Anita O'Day. I never tire of the Great American Songbook. I never tire of the country blues of Robert Johnson or the urban blues of T-Bone Walker. Never tire of funkmeisters James Brown, Sly Stone, George Clinton, the Isley Brothers, and Prince; sweet crooners Curtis Mayfield, Michael Jackson, Maxwell, and Jaheim; old gospel giants Claude Jeter and Joe Ligon; newer gospel giants Marvin Saap and Jason Nelson; poets Nas, Q-Tip, and J. Cole.

My debt to African American music is immense. Beyond leading me to God, the music has taught me style: how to sculpt stories, elongate riffs, cut off notes, go deep.

So the beat goes on. I am blessed to be working with an ever-changing cast of cool characters: Lenny Kravitz, rock-and-soul icon and brother in Christ; Desmond Child, Cuban-Hungarian-American composer of enduring rock anthems such as Bon Jovi's "Livin' On a Prayer"; Morris Day, leader of the Time and charismatic Prince accomplice; Kevin Durant, basketball superstar.

Sometimes I'm asked how I can write four or five books at once. The simple answer is that I'm sober. Rather than squander my energy, I'm able to channel my passion into creative production. Without following faith-based programs, it wouldn't be possible.

I'm a ghost who's found a groove. The essential groove has everything to do with jazz, R & B, and gospel. It's a black groove, a blues groove, but I believe it's also a cosmic groove. The groove keeps me going. To get in the groove is to get with God, where righteous rhythms are eternal. God *is* the groove.

I conclude by praising God, not because God needs or requires praise, but because the very act of praise allows me to make a kind of word music that fills me with joy. Praise is the positive voice of the heart, the passageway from fear to faith, awakening the sleeping soul so that it might sing, now and forever more.

THANKS
TO:

Beth Adams, a brilliant editor who helped give this book shape.

David Vigliano, soul brother agent.

My loving family: Roberta, Alison, Jessica, Henry, Jim, Charlotte, Alden, Jimmy, Isaac, Esther, Elizabeth, Sarah, Jeremy, Julia, Bojan.

My loving friends: Alan Eisenstock, Harry Weinger, Susan Teegardin, Herb Powell, Phil and Sue Maxwell, John Tayloe, Juan Moscoso, Ian Valentine, Tommy Swerdlow, Tavis Smiley, Charles Rosasco, Dennis Franklin, Peter Lownds, Richard Cohen, Richard Freed, Josh Sklair, Patrick Henderson, John Bryant, James Austin, Herb Boyd, Ron Lockett, Charlie Keil, Irving Feldman, and Fernando Feldman.